Pray for Mil

THE SPLENDOUR OF THE LITURGY

THE SPLENDOUR OF THE LITURGY

by

MAURICE ZUNDEL

TRANSLATED BY
EDWARD WATKIN

LONDON
SHEED & WARD
1945

NIHIL OBSTAT: ERNESTUS MESSENGER, Ph.D.
CENSOR DEPUTATUS
IMPRIMATUR: E. MORROGH BERNARD
VIC. GEN.
WESTMONASTERII, DIE 21A IUNII 1939

FIRST PUBLISHED SEPTEMBER, 1939
BY SHEED AND WARD, LTD.
110/111 FLEET STREET
LONDON, E.C.4
FIFTH IMPRESSION 1945

PRINTED IN GREAT BRITAIN
BY PURNELL AND SONS, LTD.
PAULTON (SOMERSET) AND LONDON

CONTENTS

I

THE MASS OF THE CATECHUMENS OR THE LITURGY OF THE SYNAGOGUE

II

LITURGY OF THE SUPPER
OR MASS OF THE FAITHFUL

III

FONS AQUAE SALIENTIS
IN VITAM AETERNAM

PREFACE

It is more important to make men *see* the Church in the divine purity of her inner life than to praise or defend her. She is the Mother whose catholic heart embraces the souls even of those who know her not, even of those who would destroy her. She is the Mother whose unwearied prayer rises every hour in praise or in supplication towards the most pure Beauty which alone can fill our souls, starved upon littleness, with its glory.

This book seeks to make men see the light which illumines her countenance and the dream of Beauty glowing in it, and seeing them, recognise her as the dwelling-place of the Spirit and the Bride of the Lord.

What the book has managed to capture of that pure radiance is God's share in it and the work of His grace. All its shadows and blemishes are the author's.

PREFACE TO THE SECOND EDITION

THE Oeuvre de St. Augustin at St. Maurice has often asked me to reissue this work. This request was the most charitable way of ensuring that I should improve upon the very faulty execution of the first edition.

I hope this edition will be a little less unworthy of its object. The Mass is a mystery, which must be made our living experience. And that experience is no less than a death for love. Its divine reality surpasses all words. The term ' Poem '[1] is appropriate to it only in its etymological sense of something done or enacted. The Mass is the supreme Action, the act of Redemption itself in the Memorial which makes it present.

Its fruitfulness can be perceived only by opening one's entire being and drawing together all one's powers. What Ignatius of Antioch said of the Incarnation of the Word is perfectly applicable here—' Mysteries of clamour in God's silence '.[2] The Liturgy is a school of silence. It teaches us to listen. And to listen is possibly the highest form of obedience and love. How many souls whose secret was violated by words would have been opened to their own mystery, had we heeded better God's method of action displayed in the silence of the Host.

These pages would offer the humblest testimony to this adorable reserve of the supremely Magnanimous, the

[1] In French the book is entitled *Le Poème de la Sainte Liturgie*.
[2] Eph. xix. 1.

xi

incomprehensible respect with which He treats souls, a respect that is the highest revelation of the value He attaches to the perfect freedom of our love.

It is in this silence that our soul has found her native land, and the mystery of the Church has become visible to us as the supreme demand and sublimest source of true liberty which consists in abdication of self and ' putting on ' God.

The ineffable Reality reveals Himself only to the poor in spirit whose entire being has become a silence and a listening. I ask my readers to pray that I may live this Reality better than I have managed to express it.

NEUILLY, JUNE, 1934

A SACRAMENTAL VIEW
OF THE UNIVERSE

AT THE SPRINGS OF THE BENEDICITE[1]

LIFE reveals us to ourselves as a capacity *for the Infinite*.[2]

This is the secret of our freedom. Nothing is vast enough for us. Even the immensity of astronomical space is but an image of our hunger. We rebel against every barrier and every limit inflames our desires.

This capacity for the infinite is also the source of our indigence.

A Capacity is but an aptitude to receive. A capacity for the Infinite is an infinite void which seeks satisfaction with a craving proportioned to its abysmal depths.

Obviously we do not owe this 'limitless scope of our will to our body, which is but a point in the universe. It reveals our soul and the character of the food which must nourish us. This nourishment can be found only in the invisible world, in the inner universe of Spirit.

Even my body must find entrance into this invisible sphere and bend to its immaterial demands, if an entire portion of myself is not to be debarred from the supreme fulfilment of my personality. But the invisible world frightens and dismays the body; at the mere thought

---

[1] The Benedicite is the sublime canticle of Scripture that offers to God the praise of His creatures (Dan. iii. 52–90). Twenty verses have been taken from it to compose the canticle read in the Breviary at Sunday Lauds.

[2] This capacity for the infinite obviously does not mean that we are able to comprehend Infinity and become infinite, but that only the Infinite can satisfy us, that is the finite necessarily leaves us discontented, since it always falls short of the grasp of our will for which no bound can be assigned. For it is directed to the Good, and to the Good precisely as such, and has no other motive or spring of action save the Good itself which as such admits no limit.

of the invisible world the body feels itself threatened with expropriation and clings with the greater violence to its own domain.

Failing to achieve the unity of our whole being, body and soul, in this higher sphere we strive to realise it in a lower. Transferring our hunger to sensible objects, we invest them with the infinite attraction which harmonises with the infinity of our desire. What more natural then than to yield to their promises and fall victim to their spell? How can we resist their appeal, hungry as we are for the infinite, when the infinite thus appears within our grasp? We fail to see that what fascinates and intoxicates us in such lower objects is the projection upon them of the infinite need which impels us, the beam of light cast by the spirit on the moving crest of billows which escape us. We grasp, and of what we have grasped we retain as much as a child retains who tries to seize the iridescence of a soap bubble. Our desires grow more ravenous, we refine upon our pleasure and the void within yawns wider.

At this point if we are not to perish beneath the burdensome vanity of the objects which seduce us, we must make clear to ourselves what it is that we are really in search of. For it is not they which hold us spellbound but the bright gleam of the infinite shot in the threads of their fabric. Our worst excesses, even, bear witness to our divine vocation and in the majority of cases represent only the heart's desperate aim at a happiness beyond its grasp.

What a wound, indeed, the revelation of our greatness often proves! What an unbounded resonance is imparted to our emotions by this capacity for the Infinite which is found within our nature! Our sorrows and our joys are boundless, as are our affections and our admirations. But our satisfactions prove so insecure and so hollow. Must our actions always be vain shows whose hollowness is masked by fine language? Or must we, to escape the magic of romance, admit with calm scepticism that life is nothing more than the chaotic accidents of a meaningless physics or chemistry?

Were this our inevitable doom there would be no explanation of that craving to understand which exceeds so enormously the practical uses of knowledge. Nor could we be intelligent, if the universe is unintelligible.

Science has based its entire work, a patient and heroic task, an immortal achievement of genius, on the conviction that nature can answer the questions which she compels us to ask, that even as she generates thought so she is subject to numerical order and penetrated by rationality. And though science never attains the foundation of reality she is always in search of it and drawing closer to it as she listens to the inexhaustible secrets that natural objects confide to her.

Art has always been aware that in matter there is infinitely more than matter, and has employed matter itself to express this excess. The dimensions of the sensible world expand illimitably, its outlines lose their solidity as they melt in a translucent atmosphere; and beneath innumerable features we become aware of a single Countenance, a countenance too dazzling and poignant in its intensity for our mortal eye to perceive its features.

Love is an eternal ecstasy at the cradle of life. It has been enraptured by every hope, has known every sob, has been wounded by every wound, has pursued even to death the intoxication of life. It has made its own the language of worship, so certain is it that it encounters the Infinite. But it has rarely recognised the true nature of Infinity. Like art and science love has, for the most part, allowed itself to be drawn on without grasping the nature of the magnet that draws it; and has subjected man to indescribable tortures, with man himself at once the victim and the torturer.

Art and science have usually displayed less violence. But they have often been defiled by contact with the man who pursued them, losing their translucence and docility in the tumult of his passions, until they gratified his vanity and his pride.

Mysticism has probed these wounds with inexpressible reverence and sublime compassion. It has realised that the splendid onset must recoil upon itself or be tripped up by an idol, the triumphant escape issue in a worse bondage, unless the ecstasy encounter its true object and the Infinite be clearly revealed as Another Person, One to whom the entire man can be actually surrendered with all the demands of his inner life, all the wealth of his desires, all the immensity of his heart. Another Person, but one who belongs to the spiritual order and is so interior to the soul that the created person acquires true autonomy[1] by surrendering to Him and abandoning itself to Him as to its true Self. Another within us, but not ourself, on whom our moral being can be based, in an altruism that secures its unity by the consecration it bestows.

The mystic perceives at once the divine character of the problem and the immense values at stake in these tragic

[1] By autonomy is meant spiritual independence which is complete when man has become 'one spirit with God'. (Cf. 1 Cor. vi. 17.)

errors, errors of which only a spiritual being is capable. But he knows that the soul's wounds are also the growing points of her wings and that our deepest instincts, grasped in their perfect purity and realised to the full measure of their aspiration, lead of themselves to the silent regions of prayer. He is open to all beings, and every groaning of the universe, every searching of the mind, every dream of art, all the emotions and wounds of love, find refuge in his heart. He hears all these voices in their inner resonance, he hears their *de profundis*, and their cry for God. And he understands the hidden sense of the words of the parable, as the positive goal of all these sufferings, at once their significance and their cure : ' Friend, go up higher.'[1]

You must, he tells us, pursue your search further, identify yourself more inwardly with its Objective, by effacing yourself more, surrendering yourself more profoundly, listening more humbly. For it is as the self is crucified that the Other reveals Himself within us and the Infinite to whom every being is open permits us to know Him as a spiritual Presence and an overflowing Life. Your arms must open to give, not to grasp, to offer your life, not to take possession of another's life.

And this precisely is the secret of the Cross, the mysterious birth of a new world, the tree of life planted by Divine mercy in our hearts, whose inexhaustible fruitfulness the Sacred Liturgy evokes and realises every moment of the day, somewhere on the surface of the earth.

When the Liturgy is genuinely lived, when rising up as the Divine hymn of Silence it enters the gates of the recollected soul, its power of reconciliation cannot be told. Everything bows peacefully to the redemptive demands

[1] Luke xiv. 10.

of Crucified Love. Gestures turn inwards, words become silent, chants listen, colours set forth the soul's seasons, incense bears her prayer aloft, the whole of matter offers the depths of its being to be the tabernacle of the Spirit. Creation is seen from within transparent in the living unity of Love. The Light of the world shines in the flame of a candle, its Heart beats in the mystery of the flickering lamp. In this state of contemplation the universe has become one immense sacrament.[1] We discern its three dimensions of being,[2] the limitless vista of its three orders, and thus behold it as the supreme gift of Divine Love to human, and the supreme thanksgiving of human love to Divine. The Infinite reveals its presence within reach of the spirit and at the heart of transfigured matter which can now be seen only with the eyes of the soul, and the Presence is grasped more and more as we taste the Divine Leaven which under the veil of bread incorporates into our life the ineffable mystery of Crucified Love.

Our vision pierces to the inmost centre of things and expands from within outwards as it follows the motion of its source—seeing even the surface in the inner light and spelling out God's thought in the sublime alphabet of symbols. The humblest being shines on the soul's horizon like a monstrance, and everything we meet adds another note to the Canticle of the Sun that our hearts are singing.

[1] In the wide sense of a sign which represents and in a measure communicates the Divine.
[2] Understood according to Pascal's vast conception : ' The infinite distance that separates *bodies* from *spirits* symbolises the infinitely more infinite distance that separates *Spirits* from *Charity*. For *charity* is supernatural.' *Pensées*, 793. (Br.)

HOLY WATER

THE ASPERGES

WHAT a marvellous dignity has been bestowed on water, what love, what reverence, what charity, has been displayed in regard to it!

Poets had sung of springs, of rivers and of seas. And of that water, which is the fruitful nurse of every living thing beneath the sky, they had told the wonderful course, its vast and unceasing Odyssey, accompanied by the brotherhood of the stars and the wind, under the blazing conduct of the sun and the moon's silent solicitation, to become in turn the roaring torrent and the murmuring brook, the dreaming lake and the tempestuous ocean, the mighty river and the peaceful spring, the rain pouring in heavy drops and the translucent dew cradled in the heart of the rose. They had celebrated in their songs the softness of mist and the gloom of fogs, and presented in epic strains the solemn procession of the clouds.

It might seem that water had received its meed of praise and fulfilled its destiny in these twin cycles: the cosmic and the poetic.

But a more sublime dignity is reserved for water, to be conferred upon it by the mysterious intervention of its Divine Source.

Water is a creature, and this commonplace fact is its first title of nobility. For to be a creature is to be in the thought and love of God. It is thus to participate after a fashion in God's life. But is it possible to participate in

God's life without participating in the same measure in His action?

It must needs share equally in both. Thus every being has its proper action in which a ray of the Divine Causality is operative, ordained in view of the ultimate ends of the universe for whose accomplishment every activity must co-operate. This sum total is God's goodness as it communicates to every creature the inexhaustible riches of His heart. Who shall set a limit to the outpouring of these treasures when the sole measure of the gift is infinite Love? Certainly God cannot create a being equal to Himself by its very nature. To be created implies a dependence incompatible with an infinite nature. Therefore the Divine Being is communicated in its fullness only within the bosom of Godhead, in the Generation of the Son and the Procession of the Holy Spirit. Every production of being outside God involves an inevitable limitation, restricting the span of its nature to the infinitely diverse but always limited capacities of the nature which receives it. But though this dependence is involved by the very fact of our creatureliness, from which God Himself could not dispense us without withholding existence, it would seem as though He has done His utmost to compensate us for the limitations involved and annul their effects by that marvellous elevation of our being through His grace whereby our goal is *His own* intimate life as *our* supreme Beatitude.

He has willed to dispel the shadow of our origin by the superabundance of His light. Instead of servants He has preferred to have sons, and instead of the terror of creatures crushed by the majesty of their Sovereign Lord, He has awakened in our hearts the love which responds to love, a love that is wholly His free gift.

'Henceforth I no longer call you servants ; but I call you *friends*.'[1] This appellation, though primarily addressed to spiritual beings, is, notwithstanding, extended in the plan of redeeming Love to every creature in so far as it is capable of responding to the Divine call.

Only a spirit, it is true, can consciously share the intimacy of the Divine life and give a free consent to the infinite love so mysteriously offered to our choice. But although irrational creatures cannot themselves enter the sanctuary of the Spirit, they can at least become messengers of His love and lifegiving signs of His grace.

Thus, by the gift which they bestow though unable to take possession of themselves, they partake after their fashion in the infinite sublimity of the Source, its unclouded spirituality, its most intimate love.

The Life which cannot abide in them does at any rate pass through them, and its eternal wellspring, the Blessed Trinity, thus becomes the mysterious bond and unutterable secret of *every* creature.

It is in this comprehensive sense that we may under-stand the command given by Jesus to His Apostles : ' Go into all the world and preach the Gospel to every creature.'[2]

In any case it is in this perspective that we must envisage the entire sacramental economy, in as much as it employs irrational creatures as instruments of our sanctification. They become a language whose meaning is imparted by the Word of Life for whom to say is to act. They become them-selves operative words, and the water over which the Divine Dove hovers is for the soul that submits to its operation a well of water springing up to everlasting life.[3]

[1] John xv. 15.   [2] Mark xvi. 15.   [3] John iv. 14.

It is from this point of view that we regard the sacraments as signs which effect what they represent.

We are indeed very far from forgetting the spiritual dispositions indispensable, if we would receive the sacraments profitably. The daylight does not illuminate a house if the shutters are closed. We know that God is a Spirit, and those who adore Him must adore in spirit and in truth.

Nor yet can we conceive the Divine power which the Sacraments transmit as contained *corporeally* in the sign which represents it. We reject such a conception with horror. We merely hold that in the heart of every creature there is a vestige of the Blessed Trinity, and that the most material elements possess, potentially at least, a capacity to serve spirit, a mysterious expectancy which God can one day fulfil in accordance with His plans. If with sounds, the elements of noise, we can build the fluid and diaphanous structure of music, if paper and ink can evoke in the souls of other men delicate echoes of our thought, if a kiss can reveal to a leper the most sublime charity, is it surprising that God should deign to awaken in us by a cosmic language the most intimate tones and most secret heart-beats of His own life?

Shall we take scandal and argue that He seems thus to make us subject to corporeal elements—over which nevertheless His tender love does not disdain to brood—and shall our attitude to the universe be less brotherly than His is paternal? Shall we not rather be thrilled with delight that we cannot escape His loving pursuit, and that we behold the Face of eternal Love looking up at us from every creature? For although every object is not a Sacrament in the strict sense of the term, itself moreover analogical,[1] which is the prerogative of the seven signs called by that name, every object nevertheless is or may become sacramental: a sign which communicates the Divine by representing and in a fashion provoking a birth of God's grace in our souls.

From the air perfumed by the Angelus to the humble fronds of Palm Sunday, from the mountain top lit by a Cross to the sea hallowed by a Breton Pardon, from the slow flocks blessed by the priest to the space-devouring aeroplane dedicated by prayer to righteous uses, there is nothing good that cannot be invested by the Church's blessing with the mystical halo of Divine Love.

And since whatever *is* is as such good—for evil is but privation of being—it is, in sum, the entire universe which tends to become a sacrament, as it were a vast monstrance filled with God's Presence.

New earth, transparent world, radiant springs that are the song of the Fountain, silver torrents that bear along with you the whiteness of the snow-clad summit, happy banks between which flows the river of life!

Vidi aquam egredientem de templo a Latere dextro : Alleluia. I saw water flowing from the temple on the right: Alleluia. And all those to whom that water came were saved by it and sing:

Alleluia, alleluia.

Is not water closer to you now? Do you not perceive trembling in it the mystery of the Love that gives it to you, and do you not already love it as a sister?

[1] There are degrees even in the Seven Sacraments. Baptism, for example, is not a Sacrament on the same level and in as full measure as the Holy Eucharist.

It awaits you at the entrance of the Church, the water of your baptism, the water of your purity, the water of your Divine infancy. Nor is this enough. The priest scatters it in the air with a moist wand, that it may fall upon your brow, a dew of gladness :

Asperges me Domine hyssopo : et mundabor.
Thou shalt sprinkle me, O Lord, with hyssop, and I shall be cleansed,
Thou shalt wash me, and I shall be whiter than snow.

I
THE MASS OF THE CATECHUMENS
OR LITURGY OF THE SYNAGOGUE

1. THE PREPARATION

THE SIGN OF THE CROSS

WE begin the divine Liturgy by signing ourselves with the Cross in the name of the Father and the Son and the Holy Ghost. We trace on ourselves the form of the Cross whose mystery we are about to live. We call upon the everlasting Love of which, at the cross-roads of history, the Cross is the bleeding ecstasy. We invoke the indivisible Trinity to whom this sacrifice is offered by the Sacred Humanity which subsists in the Word.

We adore the Father who expresses Himself by uttering the Word, the Word who affirms Himself by expressing the Father and the Spirit who wills Himself as the eternal flame of the kiss that unites them. We confess the mysterious fecundity of the Supreme Unity, and the infinite holiness of the relations in which the Persons consist. For here s hidden the mystery of unfathomable charity: the Divine Life does not subsist, does not issue into a personal centre, save as an outgoing towards another, and the Self of each Person is wholly ecstasy and wholly altruism; the incommunicability of the self is based upon an eternal communication, the appropriation of being is its absolute and complete gift, no selfishness is conceivable, no return upon self, no self-satisfaction and no ' possession '! The eternal purity of boundless Love discloses in the treasure of its abysses a glimpse of Poverty's holiest and most sublime Countenance.[1]

[1] In the course of this meditation we shall have frequent occasion to speak of the Poverty of God. The term is not used because we deny the infinite riches of the Divine Being to which, on the contrary, we shall often refer. It simply

We may perhaps have regarded the doctrine of the Trinity as no more than a memorised formula, or a purely metaphysical problem in which a subtle though true distinction harmonises the multiplicity of the Three with the Unity of the One.

Faith beholds it very differently from this. It beholds the mystery of eternal Holiness in the infinite altruism of an everlasting charity. This surely is suggested by St. John's words in his first Epistle. 'We know and believe the love that God hath to us. God *is* love.'[1]

Can we then be surprised that the expression in time of the Divine Life—in the Incarnation of the Word—was completed on the Cross in the anathema of the most cruel

means that these riches, instead of being appropriated 'possessively' by each Person, so as to be exclusively centred upon Him, are appropriated relatively and in an altruistic fashion by the communication of all that each Person has and *is* to the other Persons who stand in an analogous relation to Himself.

An appropriation of this kind which renders the Divine Being personal as three selves completely relative and completely unselfish, may be termed a relative appropriation, a giving and a communicating appropriation, unpossessive and dispossessing. And these terms are employed with all the spiritual undertones they possess in the language of charity whose essence is self-donation. That is to say, in other words, what each Person is, is in a sense a gift, subsisting in and by His relation to the others.

Evangelical poverty, which restricts the use and possession of temporal goods only as a means to the dispossession of self and to give birth to the poverty of a self that has become a pure outpouring of love towards God, poverty 'of spirit', finds therefore in the Blessed Trinity its ineffable source, supreme example and eternal home.

Père Garrigou-Lagrange in his work on *God, His Existence and Nature* (4th ed., p. 510) treats this point admirably : 'How is there here the least selfishness ? The self is nothing but a subsistent relation to the Object of love and appropriates nothing. . . . The Father's sole egoism is to give His infinitely perfect nature, retaining nothing for Himself but His relation of paternity, by which moreover He is essentially related to His Son. The Son's only egoism and the Holy Spirit's is the relation of both to the Father from whom they proceed. These three Divine Persons in as much as they are essentially related to Each other constitute the eminent exemplar of the life of charity.' (Cf. Maritain's analogous observations on the 'humility of God'. *Art et Scholastique.* Ed. 1927, p. 245.)

[1] 1 John iv. 16.

poverty—and in the infinite opening of the outstretched arms?

Deep calls to deep in their incomprehensible interchanges, each a reciprocal and unfathomable ' *de profundis* '.[1]

With what reverence, therefore, fervour and opening of heart and mind, with what profound wonder and joyful gratitude, with what unhasty deliberateness and complete recollection, we should make the sign of the Cross, always and everywhere, but with an even more intimate recollection, as we enter upon the Divine Liturgy.

In the name of the Father, and of the Son, and of the Holy Ghost. Amen.

[1] The *de profundis* of the Godhead banished by man, extending Its arms all day long to a people that rejects It and the *de profundis* of the Sacred Humanity made ' sin ' for us and agonising beneath the inexpressible burden of all our rejections. This of course is St. Paul's phrase. (2 Cor. v. 21). ' God hath made Him to be sin for us, who knew no sin, that we might be made the justice of God in Him.' That is, God has made Him the victim of sin by identifying Him in a sense with our sins.

JUDICA ME

I will go in to the altar of God,
To God who is the joy of my youth.

This antiphon takes us back to the time when Psalm xlii[1] was recited privately by the priest before going to the altar. It is charged with all the ardour and all the homesickness of the Psalmist in exile by the sources of the Jordan far from Yahweh's holy mountain.

It is the antiphon of the Mass, and the Mass is the ripe fruit of the tree of life planted on Calvary, the mystery of the grief that produces joy in the ascent of love.

It is so easy to say the words that signify the gift of self, so difficult to keep their promise.

When there is nothing more to receive and the hour has come to give, that is to say when love's hour has struck, we no longer recognise the Face whose presence our devotion implored. We refuse the bitter cup, we turn away from the Cross and our heart is filled with complaints against the injustice of fate.

Give judgment for me, Elohim, and decide my cause,
Against an unholy people :
Rescue me from the godless and treacherous.
For Thou, O God, art my strength.
Why hast Thou forsaken me ?
And why must I go about in sadness, humbled by my enemy ?

[1] xlii in the Hebrew Bible.

24

God understands this complaint so well that He has Himself put it into the words spoken by the inspired singer, that we may never doubt that His ear is always open to our lamentations. He never wearies of our cries who has given our human loneliness the mysterious refuge of an infinite agony : ' Father, if it be possible, let this cup pass from me.'[1] Alas, it is not always possible. There are valves so great that our heart must break to give them entrance. If the Infinite is to be incorporated into our life, it must necessarily burst its bounds.

Our being quivers with dread beneath the blows of this death which suddenly deprives us of all the familiar supports, estranging us even from our own countenance. If *only* the true Life might even so be born in us, and the soul rise from her grave into the Divine Light.

> Send forth Thy light and Thy truth
> That they may lead me
> And guide me to Thy holy mountain
> And to Thy Tabernacle.

Little by little the soul is freed from herself, and the centre of her life transferred from self to God by this gaze in which her entire being is intent.

> I will go in to the altar of Elohim,
> Of El[2] the light of my joy.

Now she thinks no longer of herself and is already steeped in that mysterious zeal for God's glory which makes every soul its humble minister.

> I will praise thee with the kinnor, Elohim, my God.

[1] Matt. xxvi. 39.   [2] El is another form of the Hebrew name for God.

Charity has found her order, to love self for God's sake, God for His own sake by an adherence to Him, free from self-interest and infinitely exceeding our happiness. Henceforward sorrow will be no longer this turning back of the soul upon herself as she entrenches herself in her sufferings, but the affliction of seeing Love ignored and His kingdom delayed. And since nothing can dam the stream of charity welling up in the silence of the heart, the springs of joy abide in the inmost centre of the soul even when they do not reach the surface and become conscious.

My soul, why art thou sad,
And why troublest thou me?
Put thy trust in Elohim. For even yet I shall praise Him.
My deliverer and my God.

So the exile ends and the soul is restored to her native land in the disinterested praise of pure contemplation.

Glory be to the Father, and to the Son, and to the Holy Ghost.
As it was in the beginning, is now and ever shall be, world without end. Amen.

CONFITEOR

WE are too prone to confine the sphere of sin to those external transgressions which offend against the accepted moral code—whose requirements grow ever fewer. Apart, moreover, from the fact that the code of social morality is often arbitrary in the extreme, blind even on such an essential matter as the just distribution of the necessities of life, it is in general completely unaware of the serious character of interior faults, and fails to see that they are the *sources* of external wrongdoing and that the only adequate cure of sin must begin at the centre of the soul. Attachment to self by turning away from God, this is the essence of the tragedy of which God Himself is mysteriously the victim. His kingdom, moreover, cannot without our consent be established in us or extended to the universe, in as much as man and nature are subject to our souls.

For this reason everything that darkens within us the splendour of the Divine Face, or diminishes the irradiation of His love, everything that intercepts the current of the grace which effects an inner contact between souls by establishing that contact between those souls and God, is a crime against the essential order of the universe.

We sometimes imagine ourselves righteous when we are unconsciously making God Himself the servant of our plans, when His Kingdom is but the pretext for our ambition and the cloak of our pride. We are no doubt more ignorant than guilty, and we may perhaps need look only to ourselves to catch a glimpse of the profundity of the evil we have done and the vast extent of the good we have omitted to do.

No, life is not confined to those external episodes accessible even to a superficial glance. On the contrary, its reality is revealed only to the supreme depths of the spirit as a mystic tragedy unfolds.

Whenever we assert self, we have in fact closed the door against God, in the darkness of a heart which refuses to allow His light to enter. For we have never less than the Infinite to give by the humility of an action through which His Presence shines.

We should indeed be guilty of most fearful sin, were we not so profoundly ignorant.

Moreover, we become aware of the hideous character of our pride only at the time and in the measure in which God at once shows us its horror and heals us of it.[1]

The keenest sense of our guilt is thus bound up with the unfailing hope of pardon, and the deepest contrition excludes all discouragement by renewing a filial trust. For

Our help is in the name of the Lord who hath made heaven and earth.

At this depth and in this light the language of an accusing conscience is obviously the only language which fits the experience of the soul; and the humility felt by the heart finds its natural outlet in a confession which calls upon the entire spiritual universe to witness sins which have offended

[1]Cf. Pascal, *Mystère de Jésus* : ' What I tell thee is a sign that I intend to cure thee.' 553 (Br.).

every creature by intercepting the light which issues from their Source.

I confess to Almighty God, to Blessed Mary ever Virgin, to Blessed Michael the Archangel, to Blessed John the Baptist, to the Holy Apostles Peter and Paul, to all the Saints, and to you, my brethren, that I have sinned exceedingly, by thought, word and deed, by my fault, by my own fault, by my own most grievous fault.

Therefore I beseech Blessed Mary ever Virgin, Blessed Michael the Archangel, Blessed John the Baptist, the Holy Apostles Peter and Paul, and all the Saints, and you, my brethren, to pray for me to the Lord Our God.

Do the faithful understand when they hear the priest make this confession that the holiness of his priesthood which he owes to Christ does not exempt him from the common weakness of men which he owes to his humanity?

They would find in this consideration a source of prayer, rather than necessarily unprofitable criticism; for prayer applies the sole efficacious remedy to any faults they may have to deplore in their priests. It is perhaps the most tragic aspect of man's destiny that sinners are called to save sinners, but also without a doubt its most marvellously redemptive aspect. For there is no more irresistible call to virtue in the world than the eyes of a child asking its father and mother a silent question, serenely confident that the question admits of but one reply: 'You do yourselves, don't you, what you tell me to do?' It is in this way that souls often reveal to us the splendour of the Face for which they look in us.

The alternation of the two Confiteors expresses in the most moving fashion this double current of mystical aid, by turn given and received in the silent hearing of the avowal and the confident intercession of prayer :

℣ May Almighty God have mercy on you, forgive you your sins, and bring you to life everlasting. Amen.

How could a prayer nourished upon humility and offered to God by charity fail to be heard ?

Certain, therefore, that the prayer is ratified in heaven ; the priest makes the sign of the cross and says :

May the Almighty and merciful Lord grant us pardon, absolution and remission of our sins. Amen.

Then deepened by contrition and revived by forgiveness, love resumes its ascent with new vigour, to the rhythm of the rapid dialogue in which alternate petitions and responses, brief and glowing like darts of fire, lay siege to the heart of God.

> Turning to us, My God,
> Thou wilt give us life,
> And Thy people shall rejoice in Thee.
> Shew unto us Thy mercy, O Lord,
> And grant us Thy salvation.
> Lord, hear my prayer
> And let my cry come to Thee.

This appeal concludes with the priest's ascent to the altar. Before he climbs the steps he addresses to the faithful people the greeting which is to rally them at every stage of the Holy Mass, and establish contact between them and the celebrant in their intimate union with Christ, the invisible celebrant in whose action the people share as truly as does the priest :

> The Lord be with you!
> And with thy spirit!

The priest raises himself from the bowing posture which his supplication has required thus far, stretches out his hands in the gesture of the ancient orante, and climbs the steps leading up to the holy table which is the Church's true sanctuary in the mystery of Faith :

Take from us our iniquities, we beseech Thee, O Lord, that with a pure heart we may enter the Holy of Holies Through Christ our Lord. Amen.

2. THE RITES OF ENTRANCE

THE LITURGICAL KISS

LIKE the sepulchre of Our Lord, the altar is alive. Death has done its work; but we are conscious of the near return of life, already hovering above its silence. Five crosses emblazon on the sacred stone the light of the five wounds. It is indeed the same Christ who once hung wounded on the Cross, who now triumphs in His glory.

To reach the Resurrection we must pass through death. We ourselves here below can support the intoxication of life only when we have come from the purifying embrace of the Cross, when the death of the heart calms our hands' ardent craving to possess. At first, no doubt, we rebel, pretend that we have not noticed the flaw in our happiness, cling desperately to the images of the possessions we have already lost. But at last we understand that it is better for us to bear sorrow than to profane joy.

Then we begin to perceive the mysterious fertility of the peace of Calvary. It is shown us in the spiritual outcome of that search for happiness which, while we sought it in the sphere of the senses (as we did so long and so obstinately),[1] left us so cruelly lacerated; and in the *interior*, and for that very reason inexhaustibly fruitful, resumption within our own souls of a quest which while we sought in the external world led only to a delusive disintegration of persons and things, divided within them-

[1] By a species of transmutation (a transformation which amounts to a change of nature) of quantity into quality.

selves and against each other. But we have an enormous climb before us, and a corresponding need to be supported by that Hope which at the Holy Sepulchre awaited the fulfilment of the Divine promises.

It was beyond death that the prayer of the agonising Christ was heard. Therefore His mysterious sojourn in Joseph of Arimathea's tomb imparts to us teaching, most human in its humility and most divine in its brotherhood.

We shall be able to accept the Cross which He carried for us—which He will carry in us—with the twofold certainty that we shall find life by consenting to lose it, and that He involves us in His death only to make us share His resurrection.

This is the meaning of the kiss that the priest, when he goes up to the altar-table, gives to Christ *lying* there under the symbol of the hallowed stone.

As on the day of his ordination he replied ' *adsum* ', present, to the Bishop's summons, pledging his entire being with no other security than the grace which called him, he continues to say every morning, more distrustful now of himself and more confident in his God's love : " Present : What do you ask of me to-day ? Shall I begin to be Thy true disciple, shall I at last share in that communion of Thy sufferings which is the choice portion of Thy friends ? Whatever you give me, Lord, give me first of all Thyself, for it is Thou whom I seek, Thou whom I hardly knew, Thou who dost draw me so powerfully, Thou who freest me from myself, Thou who art my bread and my wine."

What does a kiss mean in the mysterious language of human love but this : You are my food, the reason of my existence, the source of my life ?

That gesture is renewed here and acquires its full meaning. For it signifies the adherence of the entire man to the crucified Saviour. Here am I, to die with Thee, for Thee and at Thy hand : here am I, to live, no longer my own life but Thine. Love, it is true, always implies in its fundamental impulse this transfer of the entire being to another. But it cannot achieve it apart from God. And it is in Christ alone that love is aware of its own demands and fully realises its true nature. The Cross alone can so thoroughly dispossess a man of himself as to identify him really with another, by the free offering of a gift which regards only his true good. The most human loves have a mystical vocation. It is because they are ignorant of it that they so often issue in those appalling tragedies in which they deny themselves in their despair and torture themselves in their frenzy.

The Liturgy recalls them silently to their source by this morning kiss which buries our love in the agony and the death, the hope and the victory of the Only Son.

This surely is the moment to commit our heart to God that He may fashion it at His good pleasure ; and to renew all our affections in the fire of His Spirit.

We are not indeed called upon to give up loving but to begin to love truly. Those, moreover, who love God are those who best love their brothers, their fellow men. Their lips which retain the print of the altar can no longer profane the language of love, and their heart which has rested on the heart of the Master knows that we do not love, unless we give our life.

The Kiss of Peace in the heart of the Mass will open up these springs of divine Love and display in the greeting of the sacred ministers the spontaneous expansion towards men of charity towards God. For it is in this order that the life of the heart finds its balance, its purity and its joy. We truly give ourselves only by giving God, after having given ourselves to God. Every affection must yield place to Christ letting His love shine forth. This is admirably signified by the liturgical greeting which the priest utters oftenest after he has kissed the altar, as though first to impregnate his lips with the Divine Presence:

Dominus vobiscum
The Lord be with you.

If in all our affections we are true to the profound significance of this symbolism, we shall perceive that the Liturgy is the purest and most sublime school of love. And we shall feel the more ashamed at having loved so little and so ill, when we make our own on the threshold of the sacred Action the words accompanying the kiss of the altar:

We beseech Thee, O Lord, by the merits of Thy Saints, whose relics are here, and by the merits of all the Saints, to forgive (me) all *my* sins.

It was no doubt in this spirit that Peter, admonished of his weakness by his denial, declared in the utmost humility his love to his risen Master: ' Lord, Thou knowest all things, Thou knowest that I love Thee.'[1]

And who can say of penitent or virginal love, the love of John the Evangelist or the love of the Magdalen, which of the two is the dearer to God ?

[1] John xxi. 17.

This kiss steeped in tears, stripped by death, transfigured by the resurrection, this immaterial kiss imprinted on the sacred stone, is the Song of Songs sung in the silent heart of the Church, the purest fulfilment of the inspired love-song's ecstatic appeal:

> *Osculetur me osculo oris sui.*
> May he kiss me with a kiss of his mouth.[1]

[1] Cant. i. 1.

THE INTROIT

ALL harmony is a form of silence. We realise this when a sudden noise breaks the silence of a hot summer evening. The whole of nature was throbbing, all living things chiming together in a delirium of ruby light, the hills hymning in anthems of flame the ecstasy of the sun when suddenly a shout has broken the charm completely, a noisy brawl has made us conscious of the majesty of silence by the very act of profaning it.

All harmony withdraws us within ourselves and invests even material objects with a spiritual atmosphere which places them within the soul. Their lineaments unfold, soften, grow unsubstantial, are gathered up, efface themselves, ultimately draw light from the infinite dream which they suggest, though they can never contain it.

All the arts have made the attempt; but music more directly, perhaps, than the other arts has been able to express this dynamic aspect of reality, its openness, its movement towards the Unutterable. For this reason music has become so naturally, in the soul's highest states, the expression, the source, the sacrament of silence.[1] The Liturgy has given music an ever-increasing place. In particular it has invoked her aid to order its solemn processions, and in the first place to regulate silently the

[1] In the Liturgy at least where everything assumes in a sense a sacramental quality.

procession of the officiants from the *Secretarium*[1] to the altar, by the chant of the Introit.

Originally, about the sixth century, the Introit was an antiphonal psalm, that is a psalm divided between two choirs, one of which probably confined itself to repeating the antiphon[2] between the verses chanted by the other until the celebrant gave the signal for the Gloria Patri, the normal conclusion of all psalmody.

The simplification of rites due to the introduction of Low Mass has reduced the Introit to-day to the antiphon followed by one verse and the doxology, after which the antiphon is repeated. This is sufficient to introduce the soul into the mystery of the day. The purpose of the Introit is not primarily to give the mind an instruction, explicitly formulated, but far rather to put the soul into contact with the unutterable Presence that fills the texts. She does not need to know exactly their biblical context or weigh accurately the sense of the words. She has but to listen, her sole preparation an eager desire for light, to catch the interior music of the words, and understand that Someone is speaking to her who was waiting for her:

> The Spirit of the Lord hath filled the world and That which containeth all hath knowledge of the voice. Let God arise and His enemies be scattered. And let them that hate Him flee before His face.[3]

But what more irreconcilable enemy is there of Thy reign within me than myself? My God, withdraw me from myself beyond the tumult of my actions, beyond the noise of my words, receive within me this unformulated prayer which Thy Spirit understands better than I understand it

[1] A place of withdrawal; our sacristy.
[2] A chanted formula which served as a refrain.
[3] Pentecost.

myself, and in the inmost silence of my soul bring to birth Thy Word which contains all truth and breathes Love.

While all things were held in deepest silence and the night was in the midst of her course, Thy almighty Word, O Lord, leapt down from heaven, from Thy royal throne.

The Lord reigns, He is clothed with splendour: the Lord is clothed with strength, He hath girded Himself.[1]

He reigns, but His Kingdom is not of this world,[2] and it is useless to scan the heavens for the signs of its advent. It does not come in such fashion as to arouse the watchers, and we cannot say Lo, it is here or there. For the Kingdom of God is within you.[3]

Ye men of Galilee, why stand ye in amaze looking up to heaven? Alleluia! As ye have seen Him ascend into heaven, He shall so come. Alleluia, alleluia, alleluia.

Clap your hands all ye nations; shout unto God with cries of joy.[4]

Were you not warned: 'It is good for you that I go away? For if I go not away, the Paraclete will not come to you.'[5] What has seemingly been taken from you will be more than restored to you on the day when in your hearts you will meet with amazement your Father, your Brother and your Friend.

Receive the joy of your glory, alleluia, giving thanks to God, alleluia, who hath called you to a heavenly kingdom, alleluia, alleluia, alleluia!

---

[1] Sunday within the Octave of Christmas.
[2] John xviii. 36.
[3] Luke xvii. 20–21.
[4] The Ascension.
[5] John xvi. 7.

" How incomprihensible are his judgments and how unsearchable his ways! ,,   (Rom. II, 33)

PAUL - EMILE COUTURE

of the

FATHERS OF ST. EDMUND

Ordained
June 29, 1956

RIEMENSCHNEIDER   ETTAL / 3

MADONNA

Hearken to my law, O my people : incline your ears to the words of my mouth.[1]

No doubt this encounter will not always have the same savour, this revelation the same splendour. Corpus Christi comes but once in the year.

He fed them with the marrow of wheat, alleluia, and filled them with honey out of the rock. Alleluia, alleluia, alleluia! Rejoice to God our helper. Sing aloud to the God of Jacob.[2]

Our daily bread usually tastes more bitter. The soul must become acquainted, by living them in her measure, with all the states of the Only Son. For God cannot identify us with His Christ, unless He conform us to His Passion. Our Christmas,[3] like that of Jesus, is always, in some degree, the offertory of Calvary's sacrifice—divinely tender though the Hand always remains that seems to lie heavy upon us—that we may be sons indeed.

The Lord said to me : Thou art my Son, this day have I begotten thee.
Why have the heathen raged and the people devised vain things ?[4]

Whatever befalls us, Our Lord will not have given us less than His own portion, and we shall never be deprived of that glory which was the Poor Man of Assisi's dearly cherished inheritance.

God forbid that I should glory, save in the Cross of Our Lord Jesus Christ ; by whom the world is crucified to me, and I to the world.

[1] Tuesday in Whitsun Week.   [3] Our birth to God and His birth in us.
[2] Corpus Christi.   [4] Midnight Mass of Christmas.

I cried to the Lord with my voice : with my voice I made supplication to the Lord.[1]

Thus the Introit greets us at the entrance of the Mass. It is like a triumphal arch at the head of a Roman road, a porch through which we approach the Mystery, a hand outstretched to a crying child, a beloved companion in the sorrow of exile. The Liturgy is not a formula. It is One who comes to meet us.

[1] Feast of the Stigmata of St. Francis, Sept. 17.

THE KYRIE ELEISON

THE *Kyrie Eleison* witnesses to the former existence in the Roman liturgy, before the Introit was introduced, of an introductory litany. Indeed the vigils of Easter and Pentecost have preserved this litany which also survives in the Byzantine liturgies. Etheria, the virgin from Galicia, who visited the Holy Land towards the end of the fourth century,[1] heard the *Kyrie Eleison* sung at Jerusalem in the Church of the Anastasis by little children, whose voices were 'innumerable'. This was at the evening office of the *lucernarium*,[2] when countless tapers shed on the Holy Sepulchre a 'boundless' light and at the point in the service at which the Deacon[3] pronounced 'the names of each', that is to say made a memorial of the saints whose intercession was asked and the dignitaries or classes for whom prayer was regularly offered.

It is very probable that this invocation, repeated so often, impressed itself on the memory of other Latin-speaking pilgrims, who in increasing numbers visited the Holy Land, and that they spread its use throughout the West about the year 500.

Divorced from the petitions of which it was the refrain, and unable to supersede the *Te rogamus audi nos* which corresponded to it in the Roman Litany, the *Kyrie Eleison*

[1] Duchesne, *Origines du Culte Chrétien.*
[2] In Greek, *luchnikon :* the office celebrated when the lamps were solemnly lit. It is the origin of our Vespers. Cf. the Anglican Evensong.
[3] It must therefore have been one of those diaconal litanies still so common in the Byzantine rite.

45

served as the introduction and independent conclusion of that Litany and survived it when it had disappeared from the Mass. Originally it was repeated as often as the celebrant thought fit, no fixed number of repetitions being prescribed. The *Christe Eleison* was a variation to which St. Gregory (died 604) appealed as proof that the Roman custom differed from the Greek. It was never abandoned, and thenceforward the alternation of the *Kyrie* and *Christe* was an unalterable rule. From the beginning of the eighth century the repetitions were definitely fixed at nine, with the present arrangement by which three repetitions are consecrated to each Person of the Blessed Trinity.

This entire development was certainly not due to chance. We cannot ascribe to mere accident this survival of a Greek invocation at the beginning of the Roman Mass. At a period when Rome and Byzantium, the old Rome and the New were becoming alien, and their conflict was preparing the lamentable separation which still divides them, when on the Bosphorus Latin was already regarded as a barbarous tongue, and the language of Attica was unintelligible on the banks of the Tiber, Jerusalem 'our mother'[1] raised aloft this ensign of peace by fixing in our liturgy, as a merciful appeal for reconciliation, this response which all the Churches in communion with Constantinople have never ceased singing.

Kyrie Eleison
Lord, have mercy.

It was not only the Roman basilicas that began to be turned towards the East, prayer itself was " orientated ", and souls, like faces, looked towards the earthly cradle of the Gospel.

[1] Gal. iv. 26.

After all these centuries we inherit on both sides of the cleavage a situation we did not create and in which our prestige cannot reasonably be regarded as involved, whereas our Love of Christ suffers an intolerable wound. Must not the prayer common to both parties, a prayer which is humility's native cry, recall every Christian soul to the heart of the problem : What does Christ want of us ? When everyone, be he Oriental or Latin, will ask himself this question with his entire faith and charity, the *Kyrie Eleison* will be re-invested with its full comprehensiveness and will burst forth from all hearts as an irresistible demand for that Unity for which the Divine Shepherd prayed in His last prayer. ' That they may be one in us, Father, as Thou and I are one.'[1]

Kyrie Eleison
Have pity, O Lord, on our lacerated unity.

Only by the humility of faith and in the circumincession[2] of charity can the Countenance of Truth shine on all, that Truth which the Gospel reveals to us as a Divine Person, the eternal Logos, the Word of the Father.

What does Christ want of us ?

As we adopt this theocentric (God-centred) point of view, we shall think more of all the points in which we are still united than of those which divide us, and shall hear rather the underlying intention of words than their verbal significance, paying greater heed to the testimony which our brethren give of their living faith than to the language in which they strive to express it, language which often falls so far short of its riches.

[1] John xvii. 21–23.
[2] A mutual indwelling of souls in each other produced by the Divine Indwelling in them.

And it is only by listening to souls, letting them speak in their own words, transposing our own terminology to fit their accustomed intellectual perspective, and by constantly effacing ourselves before the Spirit who alone can teach them from within, that we shall help our brethren to answer the call of Truth. And it may well prove that we often gain more from contact with them than they from contact with us.

Certainly we must not blind ourselves to the questions which still divide us. But we shall show greater insight and more justice by emphasising the essential agreement between souls that sincerely love Christ than by giving an indiscriminate welcome to superficial observations which are often concerned with subordinate aspects of controversies that embitter existing differences, rather than with principles by which agreement on the questions in dispute might possibly be reached.

There can be no doubt that our brethren will find less difficulty in understanding that the Roman Church cannot be unfaithful to the witness she has never ceased to bear to Christ, as the living teacher in the person of Peter and his successors, if they see us readier to abdicate our life that His life may take its place.

In any case, it is holiness in all denominations which in the last resort will be the most powerful agent in reconciling Christians. It is holiness that will assuredly give effect to the prayer of our Eastern brothers, passed on to the West by Jerusalem our Mother and lately restored by our Anglican brothers in the usage, authorised in practice, of the ' Revised Prayer Book ' :

Kyrie Eleison
Christe Eleison
Kyrie Eleison.

3. THE ANGELIC HYMN

THE GLORIA IN EXCELSIS

Glory to God in the highest, and on earth peace to men of good will.

THIS is the message of Christmas, given at the dawn of Redemption, the Divinely simple promulgation of the intrinsic law of reality.

For our life is in its fundamental orientation mystical. We have already remarked it. Our thirst for freedom and our need of *space*, even our rebellions and our excesses, reveal our capacity for the Infinite and our Divine vocation.

By activities without number and under diverse names we seek in every direction the fulfilment of those *unbounded possibilities* which nothing can exhaust, save He who has no bound.

The charm of infancy and the intoxication of love, the ecstasy of the artist and the passion of the investigator, the impulse of science and the development of technical invention : all these in different ways disclose these depths or attempt to fill them.

The struggle of classes and the rivalry of nations, the economic war and the conflict of states, the tragedies of money or the flesh, reveal the same abysses, testifying by their very inhumanity that it is only in what we make of ourselves that we can truly fulfil our nature, in the mystery of the interior life and a communion of spirit.

A material space, however vast, will always be too narrow a field for the expansion of infinite energies. They must inevitably explode there and inflict upon us wounds which are the fiery stigmata of the Presence we have ignored. Nor can there be any remedy for our ills so long as we acquiesce in their first principle and remain deaf to the appeal of the Spirit, keeping God exiled from our soul, our house or our city. Fearful as they are, physical catastrophes and conflicts between men are but symbols of the infinite tragedy enacted in the depths. The evil from which we suffer is, in truth, deeper than all our visible woes and all our deeds of bodily violence. It is the love of a God that bleeds in our hearts.

We bear within ourselves a supreme value which is not ourself and to which everything that is ourself ought to yield place. Our life possesses no worth, save in so far as it loses itself in Another, who is closer to us than we are to ourselves. Our sole duty, as it is our highest glory, is to prepare for Him in our own soul and in the souls of our brethren the mystic cradle in which our love shall give Him birth.

'Whosoever doeth the will of my Father who is in heaven,' Jesus said, ' he is my brother, my sister and my mother.'[1]

He is my mother. Surely the immensity of man's task could not find a more tragic expression: the task of humanity is to give birth to God.[2]

The world is not a pageant to gaze upon but a task to

[1] Matt. xii. 50.

[2] In our hearts, Our Saviour, the Venerable Bede pointed out, approved in the most felicitous terms the woman's exclamation, blessed is the womb that bore thee, when he declared that not only was she blessed who had merited to be the physical mother of the Word of God, but those also are blessed who conceive the same Word spiritually, by the understanding of Faith, and by the practice of good works, bear Him and, as it were, feed Him both in their own heart and in the heart of their neighbour. (Common of Our Lady, Noct. 3, Lesson 9.)

accomplish, a creation to achieve, a captive God to set free.

"I stand at the door and knock. If any man hear my voice and open the door I will enter." [1]

And the riddle of the world will be solved: a world in which man himself is a stranger, so long as God has not yet entered.

Why then should we complain that matter escapes us, when we multiply without limit the exterior organs of a life whose source and rule are in the spirit and which masters its tools only in so far as it takes possession of itself, by surrendering itself to One who is better than itself?

And why should we be surprised at the spectacle of these hosts of young men whom a tragic duty obliges to learn to inflict death in order to save life? For this is but the effect of a cause which we must seek elsewhere.

No doubt we shall never sufficiently execrate war. We shall never protest enough against this abominable method of solving disputes between human beings, disputes nearly always concerned with material interests, by wholesale massacre. But we must not blind ourselves to the fact that to accept the supremacy of material values, as in practice we do, renders war inevitable and is responsible for the desperate issue when innocent individuals take up arms against others equally innocent while cursing the fate that compels them to do so.

Even less than the actions of individuals can the actions of nations aim at a void. The more perfect therefore their

[1] Apoc. iii. 20.

c

organisation, the more fruitful their industry and the intenser their effort, the more unbounded and sublime their field of action should be. If then the desire for greatness is given an outward direction, there is no conquest that will not seem a duty, no attempt to mobilise the Absolute for the service of human ambition that will not appear legitimate. The entire world will not suffice to satisfy the appetite of such an ambition, which gains an illusory prestige and sacredness from being communal and not individual, and is rendered even more tragic by the needs that support it and the devotion that serves it. If the universe has bounds, the heart has none.[1] Ambition must therefore be given an object in harmony with its magnitude, a task worthy of itself. Otherwise mankind will never cease tearing itself to pieces.

In truth, there neither can nor ought to be Peace, if man does not transcend his humanity, if he does not surrender to the Infinite that importunes him, and if all nations on their knees do not meet as brothers in the common service of God's kingdom. May we not hope to witness shortly this salutary revolt of the nations against rulers who turn them away from their *human* life, by involving them in material enterprises in which they lose their earthly being without having even had the opportunity to discover their spiritual? But this revolt must begin in your own heart and be spread in the hearts of your brethren by the resources of your own. For its object is not to slay or wound, but to give life and save.

Just imagine a humanity that no longer toiled for its petty homicidal pleasures but loved unselfishly, hungered

[1] By its space the universe contains me and engulfs me as a point, by my thought I contain the universe. Pascal, *Pensées*, 248.

for God's glory and sought to see in every face a new
revelation of the eternal beauty.

What a conquest it would be, what a dream, or rather
what an inexpressible reality, what an advance in depth,
and what a peaceful victory, if you would but genuinely
believe the words you utter, and would but put your
entire soul into the praise to which the Church invites
you, in her *Gloria*, that it may be Christmas in the world,
through your heart, to-day.

> Glory to God in the highest,
> And on earth peace to men of good will.

Now therefore in company with all the sentinels of
praise on Sion's walls, with all the psalmists and all " God's
singers ", with all the heralds of the Divine glory, with
all the poor in spirit, fill with your life these most humble
words, these words modest, joyous, exultant, which
alternate like the quick responses of children's hands as
they beat out the measure to which they are dancing.

> We praise Thee,
> We bless Thee,
> We adore Thee,
> We glorify Thee.

Four ejaculations, which press forward and hasten to
lose themselves in the vast rhythm, like the flight of a
bird hovering over an abyss of light.

We give Thee thanks for Thy great glory,

for it is Thy glory that makes us aware of the infinite
distance which Thy love crossed, Thou generous One,

who canst but give ; Father of infinite majesty, whose greatness never failing always pours down upon us.

Lord, God, Heavenly King, God, the Father Almighty.

And Thou of Thy free will, the great Pauper, who art the mysterious penury of Love offering Himself to our choice in the eternal expectation of the silence in which we freely choose :

Lord God, only begotten Son, Jesus Christ.

Thou who hast entered our history, Son of man, workman and condemned criminal, Thou who hast entered our history that it may attain its summit, the supreme holiness, the baptism of blood, of Thine own sacrifice :

Lord God, Lamb of God, Son of the Father.

Thou who didst lower thine eyes in the presence of the adulteress that Thou mightest not increase her confusion :

Thou that takest away the sins of the world, have mercy upon us.

Thou who didst give the woman of Samaria living water by revealing the Gospel of the Spirit to her who was living in the flesh :

Thou that takest away the sins of the world, receive our prayer.

Thou who didst accept the Magdalen's ointment, permitting to her to follow Thee to Calvary and calling her by her name, before Thou didst ascend to Thy Father :

Thou that sittest on the right hand of the Father, have mercy upon us.

Have mercy upon us, giving what our soul entreats from Thee the poverty of a self which renounces itself and the glory of a life that expresses Thine. For to be holy is simply to permit Thee to be completely Thyself in us :

> For Thou only art Holy,
> Thou only art Lord,
> Thou only art most high :
> Jesus Christ,

in the eternal Charity that gives Thee the Father by giving Thee to the Father, Jesus our Brother and our Lord, God ever blessed :

> With the Holy Ghost
> In the glory of God the Father. Amen.

4. THE MASS OF THE CATECHUMENS STRICTLY SO CALLED

THE COLLECT[1]

PRAYER is the soul's breath, the creature's fiat in response to the Creator's in that mysterious exchange which makes us God's fellow-workers. Its purpose is not to inform God of needs which He knows infinitely better than we do ourselves, nor to move His will to satisfy them, for His will is the eternal gift of infinite Love. Its sole object is to make us more capable of receiving such a gift, to open our eyes to the light, to throw open the portals of our heart too narrow to give access to the King of glory. There is no need to importune God for our happiness, for He never ceases to will it. It is we who place the obstacle in its way and keep His love at arm's length.

Jerusalem, how often would I have gathered thy children, as a hen gathers her chickens beneath her wings, and thou wouldst not.[2]

This surely is the most poignant expression of the Divine Tragedy: 'I would, I, thy Lord and thy God—but thou, thou wouldst not.' If we place this complaint side by side with the text already quoted from the Apocalypse, 'I stand at the door and knock', we must

[1] Collecta: understand plebs, that is to say the synaxis, the assembly or gathering. This prayer was originally said at the church where the faithful assembled before leaving in procession for the church where the Station was held, and was no doubt repeated on their arrival there, thus beginning the series of Mass prayers. Cf. Adrian Fortescue, *The Mass*, 2nd ed. p. 324; also Batiffol, *Leçons sur la Messe*, 8th edition, pp. 120–121.

[2] Matt. xxiii. 37.

conclude that God always hears man's prayer, that He is the eternal answer to prayer, and that it is man who too often refuses to hear God's prayer.[1]

And prayer is precisely the response to Love's eternal invitation, which is made with an infinite regard for our freedom. It is, therefore, superfluous to ask whether every prayer is heard. It is heard if and in so far as it is a genuine prayer. For genuine prayer is the opening of the soul[2] to the mysterious invasion of the Divine Presence, and it is completely summed up in the final appeal of the Apocalypse: 'Come, Lord Jesus.'[3]

This does not mean that God's gift is strictly measured by our actual dispositions, that is to say by our immediate readiness to respond. In drawing an angle, the sides may be prolonged indefinitely when the degree of angularity is given. But there must be an angle of some degree. If, moreover, we suppose this degree capable of increase, there is nothing to prevent the angle being widened in proportion to the prolongation of the sides. Similarly in the spiritual order, given a certain degree of aperture in the soul, God's reply to ours (for in this dialogue He always takes the initiative) possesses all the freedom of an action literally inexhaustible in the means at its disposal, and effected in a fashion wholly interior. His light, though never compelling us, can exert a supremely powerful pressure upon the most intimate springs of the soul's action, and mature indefinitely that initial response which took shape in our prayer, and by which we began to answer the unutterable groans of His Spirit. It remains true that

[1] Cf. Pascal, *Mystère de Jésus*: 'Jesus has entreated men and has been refused.'
[2] An opening which every prayer should after its fashion enlarge.
[3] Apoc. xxii. 20.

there is no conversation without answers, no marriage of love without mutual consent. And it is a marriage of love that is to be concluded between God and ourselves. In this marriage whose intimate union must continually grow until its flower unfolds in eternity, prayer is our assent. There is no need to put it into words. It may be confined to a silent adherence, a simple look in which we give our entire being a calm silence in which, without adding anything of her own, the soul listens to Him who utters Himself within her by His single Word. And all prayer tends towards this transparent passivity which exposes the diamond of our free will to the rays of the eternal light. We can pray without asking for anything and without saying anything, that God may express Himself the more freely.

But we can also pray by putting into words a petition, an act of praise or thanksgiving, by murmuring a confidence or a confession by uttering our grief, our penitence, or our despair. Nothing is more unfettered, more varied, richer or more unpredictable than this conversation of love permanently carried on between God and the soul. Any one of our *needs* can serve as a support to the flight of prayer. For each is in its fashion a revelation and, so to speak, a sacrament of that need of God who in every need discloses depths which He alone can fill. It is in fact He who in every need is its inexhaustible disquiet, its wound always sensitive, its insatiable desire and its mysterious fulfilment. However material it may appear on the surface, we have but to open it up to God and loose the grip of self, and it will disclose its true nature and spread its wings in the blue.

We may ask God for anything. For whatever we ask, if we ask as we should, it is for God Himself that we ask,

and for everything which can lead us to Him, to the extent
to which it does so. Our prayer leaves God to judge of
this, content if only His Kingdom come and He is glorified
in us as He should be glorified.

The hour will indeed come when prayer, inspired by
the charity whose centre is God, and wholly cleansed of
alloy, wills God alone ; God in Himself, God in us, God
in all things. Its sole desire then will be to adhere to all
that God is in Himself, to all that He wills to be in us
and in every creature, infinitely beyond what we shall ever
be able to understand, infinitely beyond any profit we shall
ever be able to receive from it.

It is ultimately for the sake of God that the soul desires
her own Beatitude, that no obstacle may thwart His love,
that the world may realise its spiritual vocation, and that
throughout creation all may be yea, as all is yea in God.[1]

We must not be deceived by the anthropocentric
(man-centred) appearance of most prayers in books, not
excepting the Bible, the Missal, the Breviary and, even
more, the Ritual.[2] Our wants provide a ground from
which it is easy to take off. But it is to begin a flight
on which no landing will be made and whose course God
alone knows. The *Collects* of the Roman liturgy possess
this dynamic quality in the fullest measure.

At first sight they disappoint us by their lowliness, like
the Bread of Communion. They seem fashioned of our
wants.[3] But their very sobriety forbids us to stop at their
verbal surface. The soul has but to let herself go and she
is launched on the open sea voyaging over abysses of light

[1] 2 Cor. i. 19.
[2] Which contains, amongst other forms, formulas of blessing.
[3] Particularly in the Sanctorale, which, however, contains gems of the first
water.

and darkness, of sorrow and peace. They are more than prayers, they are sacraments of prayer, formulas that induce the essential prayer which we have attempted to describe. Nothing could be simpler or more bare, purer or briefer, more flexible or more compact, than these four or five phrases, harmoniously balanced, which compose the majority of our collects.

Almighty and everlasting God, mercifully look upon our weakness, and to protect us stretch forth the right hand of Thy Majesty.[1]

We are, however, well aware that the greatest dangers come from within and that no calamity can impoverish a soul that is God's temple.

Incline thine ears to our prayers, we beseech Thee, O Lord, and by the grace of Thy visitation enlighten the darkness of our minds.[2]

It is not so much that we crave to be consoled, though we are in such great need of the dew of heaven. The soul looks farther than herself, when, urged by love, she aspires to identify herself with the one model in whom humanity subsists in the Word and expresses nothing but the Word.

O God whose only begotten Son hath appeared in the substance of our flesh, grant, we beseech Thee, that by Him, whom we have beheld in our outward likeness, we may merit to be reformed within.[3]

It takes nothing short of the experience of a lifetime to disclose the significance of such a prayer. God knows

[1] Third Sunday after the Epiphany.   [3] Octave of the Epiphany.
[2] Third Sunday in Advent.

what this conformity with ' the Man of sorrows '[1] will involve for each one of us, before we behold the ' countenance of delight '[2] God alone knows our cross, as He alone can reveal it to us without wounding what is most unutterable in us. And He alone can give it us without destroying anything that deserves to survive, and can make us die without killing us. The woman who bears a child knows this inexpressible mixture of life and death, of suffering and joy in the fruitfulness of love. What can we say of the soul to whom God has given birth when it is she who must give birth to God,[3] by yielding her life as a refuge to the Life in whom all is life? She knows not whither to flee, nor whether she ought to implore a truce to her pangs by relaxing her co-operation with God's work, nor whether she dare ask Him to complete it in her by a more fearful banishment.

But he knows the soul's anguish infinitely better than herself. Is He not infinitely more a mother than any mother? For what better can we ask Him, than what He knows and wills in excess of all we ourselves could desire ?

Almighty and everlasting God, who in the abundance of Thy loving-kindness dost give beyond the merits and desires of Thy suppliants, pour forth Thy mercy upon us, forgiving that of which our conscience is afraid, and bestowing what our prayer dares not ask.[4]

A moment comes when the soul is at last so stripped of herself that she wills nothing save the will of God. This is supreme poverty and true childhood. Then she

[1] Isa. liii. 3.
[2] Ord., *Commendationis animae*.   Third Prayer.
[3] See note above, p. 47.
[4] Eleventh Sunday after Pentecost.

can begin to play before God every day, like the eternal Wisdom.[1] And everything becomes joy for her in the company of the Three who are now her family and her home.

Beyond question the end of all is like the beginning : *Joy*. The Cross has its place in the interval when the ramparts of self are demolished that the tree of life may spread its branches freely, and love attain its full stature.

Suffering is not good as such, but solely because it opens up in us the ' spaces of love '. It is good when God gives it to us. But joy is even more desirable, when it comes from Him. What is essential is to receive everything from His hand, breathing in His Spirit and listening to His Word in the silence of self.

O God, who turnest all things to the good of them that love Thee ; implant in our hearts an invincible love of Thee ; that desires, conceived by Thine inspiration, be not shaken by any temptation.[2]

We shall never exhaust the fruitfulness of these formulas which contain the most living and most sublime theology.

Nevertheless they are for every day, are suited to every condition, and teach every soul to utter what of herself she could never have expressed, calling her to the open sea, with a calmness so confident that it prevents all fear, as it excludes all excitement. The same voice invites us that summoned Peter to the deep.

' Launch out into the deep and let down your nets for a draught.'

' Master, we have toiled all night and have taken nothing. Nevertheless *at Thy word* I will let down the nets.'[3]

---

[1] Prov. viii. 30.
[3] Luke v. 4-5.
[2] Votive Mass to ask for Charity.

THE EPISTLE

CHRISTIANITY is not so much man's search for God, as God's search for man. The Divine initiative is seen everywhere. It does not, however, detract from our activity but on the contrary assures its full scope and fruitfulness.

The more sublime and beneficent an influence, the more intimately is it incorporated into our own action, and the freer it leaves us. The man of genius does not suppress our thinking, but matures it and liberates it from its shackles. In like manner the saint renders living within us the Reality of which we possessed but the notion, not the experience, and makes us desire to live it as personally as he does. Such is the operation of every *spiritual* cause when it is exercised morally.

Hence our liberty is in direct proportion to God's action upon us. In consequence of an apparent verbal opposition, transcendence[1] and immanence have been falsely opposed and the supernatural dreaded as a threat to the autonomy (independence) of the moral life. God, however, is *transcendent* in virtue of the supreme *immanence* of His nature. In the sphere of supra-sensible realities, in which we are now moving, the degree of immanence is measured by the degree of spirituality.[2] And since God's spirituality has no limit, His mmanence is equally unlimited. God is *pure immanence*. Every creature on the contrary is, so to

[1] The character of that which exceeds all categories of created being, all limitation and all definition.
[2] Or immateriality.

speak, exteriorised[1] by the intrinsic limitations of its being. It is therefore the more external to God and to itself, as its capacity for being is the more restricted. It is this lack of immanence that makes it impossible for any creature to behold unveiled, with the sole resources of its nature, Him in whom it lives and moves. However perfect it may be, it remains of itself confined to the realm of semblances. It conceives what God is by the aid of what He is not. An immediate grasp must be supernatural.

If we are nevertheless called to attain it, this vocation can be fulfilled only by an operation infinitely more interior than the most sublime spiritual operation of the created order left to its own resources. The Divine Immanence must be communicated to the intimacy of our spirit like a mysterious leaven, and the latter by an indescribable magnetism be brought to coalesce after a fashion with the Former. That is to say, the immanence, the interiority of God's *supernatural action*,[2] is guaranteed by the very transcendence of His being, as, moreover, it is the supreme manifestation of the pure immanence of His nature, since His transcendence is His immanence.

It hardly needs pointing out that God alone can initiate

[1] Every creature is a mysterious composition of light and shadow. God is pure light. He is therefore perfectly diaphanous (transparent) for and interior to Himself, whereas we remain always a mystery to ourselves and (a fortiori) He to us. He transcends infinitely our mind, though He never ceases to be most intimately present (immanent) to us. He is always present indeed, but we are not. Our shadow makes us alien to His light and sets a naturally insuperable obstacle to any immediate grasp of His essence. Grace and revelation aim precisely at removing this obstacle, by increasing our light under the influence of His, so that we may discover His presence and feed upon It. The whole process of His supernatural action (supernatural relatively to us) is therefore tending towards our highest interiority and unity, transparence and simplicity) freedom and autonomy.

[2] Supernatural in us and relatively to us. There is nothing supernatural in God and relatively to Him. The immanence of the Divine action in us is in direct proportion to God's transcendence relatively to us.

such an elevation, that is to say, such an interiorisation of our nature. For He alone can dispose of His inner life, as He alone can impart its secrets to us. It follows of necessity that if our lives even here on earth should be directed towards this immediate perception of God with the boundless intimacy it involves, we must be initiated into the Divine Life by a revelation.

This also has been regarded as an encroachment upon our spiritual independence. The objectors have lost sight of the fact that such a revelation must be addressed to the inmost region of our intellect, infinitely beyond any knowledge of which our mind is naturally capable. They have forgotten that words in so far as they are indispensable to a revelation, social in character and ordering a universal experience, must be understood in a sense beyond their ordinary significance, as themselves steeped in an inexpressible *interiority* of which the intellect unenlightened by faith, that is to say, without this new vision turned towards the Divine aspect of things, cannot form any true conception.

Men have taken texts and believed it sufficient to read them like any other document. In exactly the same way they have confused the Eucharistic Bread with common bread. In both cases faith alone can make the distinction. The same attitude, therefore, is required for approaching the Doctrine as for approaching the Sacrament. The Doctrine is also bread, a Eucharist whose mystical substance is accessible only to a vision rendered interior by the Divine Light. It is, so to speak, a sacrament whose reality, though signified and communicated by words, is always in the last resort that which is most intimate in God, that which no word can utter, no idea represent; that which will remain incomprehensible, even throughout eternity; that is to say, if by comprehension we mean an understanding adequate to its object.[1]

This is the culmination of faith. This is the abyss towards which it hastens, in which words fail, ideas become unsteady and the eyes are blinded by excess of light, and where love alone achieves a firm grasp by a wholly disinterested adherence to this overwhelming plenitude which is the incomprehensible excellence of the beloved Being.

The movement of faith must end in charity.[2] The Divine secrets it hears become fully intelligible only in the intimacy of love. Of itself faith can but point to God, tell us of every dogmatic statement: He is there but beyond the veil. Charity beneath every word perceives His Presence, and in the message delivered by faith attaches itself to the Godhead that is its author rather than to the similitudes which represent by vast outlines of shadow the eternal splendour of His light.

This is why charity abides for ever. It does not adhere to God still 'remote', as does faith which knows 'in a mirror and enigmatically'. But through this knowledge which at every moment proclaims its impotence and, so to speak, reaches out beyond itself, charity adheres to God as He sees Himself[3] in that eternal vision whereby He 'searches the deep things of God', in an infinite comprehension adequate to Himself, whose fullness will never be attained even by the glorified vision of the creature. For even the beatific vision does not know the Divine

---

[1] St. Thomas, i, xii. 7.
[2] St. Thomas, 2a, 2ae IV, and 1a and 2ae LXVI. 6.
[3] Cf. St. Thomas, 1a, 2ae LXVII, 6 ad. 2. '*Nota quod ibi negatur charitatis objectum esse Deum cognitum, dicitur esse Deum ABSOLUTE.*' Cajetan.

Nature as much as it is knowable.[1] Our Love, therefore, will possess for all eternity the joy of attachment to God in Himself and for Himself and *in His very incomprehensibility* : such however as the beatific vision will enable us to grasp it.

Saint Paul who had contemplated ' what the eye hath not seen, nor the ear heard, neither hath it entered the heart of man ', has hymned this eternity of love in the New Testament's Song of Songs, the thirteenth chapter of the first Epistle to the Corinthians.

' If I speak with the tongues of men and of angels,
but have not charity,
I am become as sounding brass or clanging cymbal.
And if I have the gift of prophecy
and comprehend all mysteries and all knowledge ;
and if I have all faith, so as to displace mountains,
but have not charity,
I am nothing.
And if I bestow in doles all my goods,
and if I deliver my body to the flames,
but have not charity,
it profiteth me nothing.
Charity is patient, is kind
Charity envieth not, is not pretentious,
is not puffed up, behaveth not amiss,
seeketh not her own, is not provoked,
regardeth not evil ;
rejoiceth not over wickedness but rejoiceth with the truth :
beareth all things, believeth all things,
hopeth all things, endureth all things.
Charity faileth never :
whereas prophesyings, they shall have an end ;
tongues, they shall cease ;
kno ledge, it shall have an end.

[1] St. Thomas, 1a XII. 7. Cf. St. John of the Cross. Spiritual Canticle. Stanza 13 with his commentary.

For we know in part, and we prophecy in part;
but when the perfect is come, what is in part shall have an
end.
When I was a child, I spoke as a child, I felt as a child, I
thought as a child;
now that I am become a man, I have made an end of childish
ways.
For now we see in a mirror, obscurely,
but then face to face.
Now I know in part; then shall I know fully,
even as I have been fully known.
So there abide faith, hope, charity, these three;
but the greatest of these is charity.'

This is the Epistle for Quinquagesima, the most sublime
expression of the theocentrism,[1] and the perfect interiority
of the Christian life. Nothing is of any value if our love
does not adhere to Love. All good works are but signs
expressing and engendering Love.

We are thus equally removed from the heteronomy[2]
of a commandment which remains wholly external and
the pretended autonomy[3] of a law determined solely by
our own will. For it is by the inmost centre of our will
that we surrender ourselves to Another who is more
internal to us than we are to ourselves. For what is more
internal to any being than its love and the object of its
love? It can find itself no longer save in this other with
whom its heart is identified; it can recover its being only
by giving it, it is not fully itself unless its disposition is
one of pure unselfishness.

Obviously God alone can be the true Object of such

[1] The attitude which takes God's point of view in everything, making God
the centre.
[2] The character of that which receives its law from another.
[3] The character of that which receives its law from itself.

self-abdication, from which it follows that even the love of our neighbour must have its centre in God, and that there is no genuine charity apart from the theocentrism[1] implanted in our hearts ' by the Holy Spirit given unto us '.[2]

Let us then restore at last to this word charity its Divine dignity, remembering that it is the name of God and expresses His entire Being. ' We have known,' wrote St. John,[3] ' and have believed the Charity that God hath for us : God is Charity.'[4]

---

[1] Not necessarily a conscious and explicit theocentrism but a practical theocentrism.

[2] Rom. v. 5.

[3] I John iv. 16.

[4] Here we translate Agape by Charity, as also above in 1 Cor. xiii. Elsewhere we translate it by love. In the Christian vocabulary the two words mean the same and are interchangeable. They always signify that most spiritual and most disinterested movement of the heart of which the Holy Spirit is the centre and the goal.

THE GRADUAL[1]

WORDS are signs of things. But what are things themselves? We agree about their practical aspect, and a language increasingly universal expresses their utility, their point of contact with our needs. But what are they in themselves?

The majority have neither the intellectual curiosity nor the leisure to inquire. Most men, however, are interested in the explanations given them, a proof that practical utility does not suffice to nourish their thought.

Investigators return again and again to the problem, continually striving to reduce the infinite complexity of the universe to some ultimate element governed by a universal law: for example, atoms of matter in motion distributed in accordance with the requirements of gravity, or 'fields of forces identical with curved spaces'.

But however they analyse phenomena they seek to attain a simple view which will satisfy their need for intelligibility.[2]

The result of extremely complicated calculations often seems, it is true, very meagre, and to tell us about the composition of the canvas and the paint rather than about the art of the picture. The entire world of values, the domain of quality to which consciousness is so acutely sensitive, seems excluded from this scientific view of the universe. This, however, is in reality but a semblance, a

[1] From *gradus*, the step, the *ambo* adjoining the Sanctuary from which it was chanted by the Deacon as a solo, the choir repeating the final verse.
[2] Cf. Einstein, *How I See the World*.

semblance, however, of which scientists themselves are often the dupes. Nevertheless the material representations which they reach satisfy them only by their coefficient of intelligibility,[1] which is a demand and a discovery of their mind, an *interior* datum, intangible and imponderable.

The eye is one thing, its vision another, and it is the look in eyes which we notice, the reflection of the soul within at this material point, on which we fix our gaze. In the same way the scientist submits phenomena to his intelligence, only in order to discover their latent *rationality*. A mysterious thought pervading the universe, present everywhere, and nowhere to be completely captured, is the very soul of his researches. He proceeds in its company and submits to its evidence, bows to its demands and is enraptured by its mystery. He surrenders himself to it even to the sacrifice of his life, and when he cries Eureka, ' I have found it ', it is because this thought has shown itself more plainly to him by the illumination it has produced in his mind.

The public knows nothing of this silent dialogue in which the mind of the scientific investigator listens to the invisible Wisdom.[2]

Technicians present the public with its results in a practically useful shape, and popularisers explain its material result. But its essence remains always untold, being, in fact, inexpressible.

Be it said to the honour of the scientific genius, that it is in this immaterial contact with the mysterious spirit-

---

[1] That is to say, by the light they produce in their mind and the support they yield to intuitions which infinitely transcend them. Cf. Pierre Boutroux, *L'Ideal scientifique des mathematiciens*, pp. 203-205. The conception of LAW which from top to bottom dominates the hierarchy of the natural and physical sciences (ibid., ps. 205–206) is qualitative in character and renders intelligible scientific conceptions whose aspect and expression are most material.

[2] Einstein, loc. cit.

uality of the universe, in thus obeying its unconstrainable attraction, and in this silent attention to its dumb confidences that the masters of science have found their purest joys and noblest consolations. It is by this communion with the unutterable that they have been able to share in their fashion the transport of the mystics, and experience the lyric rapture of the poets.[1]

They are all at bottom, in virtue of their fundamental attitude, and to the degree to which they efface themselves before the object of their quest, of the same race and the same spirit. We are speaking of the greatest men, and not primarily of their works but of their life and of the moment when the spark kindled and the encounter occurred.

They are indeed made to understand each other in silence, the scientists, the mystics and the poets, though words often separate them when they begin to speak the language of the world in general.

But words themselves can become living. Each may understand them from his own spiritual level, fill them with his experience and put into them the beating of his heart. Then language unfolds to the man who is able to hear its latent tones, and brings with it those surges of light where thought is cradled.

What really matters about words is not their strictly defined meanings which we find in the dictionary, but the imponderable aura wherein the unutterable presence in which all things are steeped, is faintly perceptible.

[1] We are thinking of the attitude of a Pierre Termier for example. We are well aware, however, that the scientist as such, who, however, is an abstraction, is not a mystic. But the man who is a scientist, like every soul, is subject, whether he knows it or not, to the mysterious soliciting of grace. If he is obedient to its motion, as we are presuming here, his scientific attitude itself will be crowned by a supernatural attraction and a mystical orientation towards the Truth as It is in itself. We would say the same of the poet.

That is why the highest state of language is poetry in which the images and the rhythms concentrate in a transparent sonority the suggestive power of words, allowing all that lies beyond to become visible.

Music completes the process by abandoning all definite significance to express only the unutterable aspect of the universe. It is therefore easy to understand why poetry and music meet in the heart of the Liturgy, as though in answer to the invitation of their Source; poetry and music which lose self-consciousness and forget themselves in humble adoration; poetry and music that contemplate and listen; interior poetry and music that calm, elevate and purify the most secret regions of the soul.

It is in the silent spaces which poetry and music open within us that the doctrinal formulae can be heard with their amplest resonance.

It was therefore natural to invoke their aid after the reading of the Epistle. For its message must be allowed to bear fruit in our personal meditation until we make contact with the Presence with which the texts are filled. We must hear this single Word which is their true meaning and which no human word can express.

The chanting of the Gradual provides this interval of silence and this time of rest in which the teaching just received can unfold in prayer, in the sweet movement of the Cantilena distilling in neums of light a divine dew.

> Hearken, O daughter, and behold,
> Bow thine ear,
> For the King hath desired thy beauty.
> In thy grace and thy beauty
> Go forth, advance prosperously and reign.[1]

[1] St. Cecilia, November 22.

But how can I, O Lord, being such as I am, endure, without dying, the glory (and the shame) of Thy choice?

> Cast thy care upon the Lord
> And He shall nourish thee Himself.
> When I cried to the Lord,
> He heard my cry
> In their sight who drew nigh unto me. [1]

Did I not give drink to the people in the wilderness, sustain the famished Elias till he came to Horeb, feed David on his flight with the loaves of the Sanctuary? I believe it, Lord, and thy prophet teaches it to us:

> The eyes of all wait upon thee, O Lord,
> And Thou givest them their food
> In due season.
> Thou openest Thine hand
> And fillest every living thing with blessing. [2]

But whence then is the unknown wound I feel, this solitude like a shoreless ocean?

> The anguish of my heart is enlarged,
> Save me from my sorrow, O Lord,
> Behold my humiliation, behold my striving,
> And forgive all my sins. [3]

I have taken thy lamentation into my own, brother, thy sorrow has made my agony heavier, I have assumed thy grief, and like thee, I have sought help and not found it.

---

[1] Third Sunday after Pentecost.   [3] Second Sunday in Lent.
[2] Corpus Christi.

> All ye who pass by the way
> Behold and see if there is any grief like unto mine.
> Having loved His own that are in the world,
> He loved them unto the end.[1]

Consent to suffer for thy brethren, fulfil in thyself what is wanting to My passion, that is, the adherence of thy love that makes it fruitful in you, that in thy heart the Cross may spread its arms, the tree of life.

> Let thy springs be poured out,
> And distribute thy waters over the public places.
> Happy is the man that can shew mercy
> And freely lends :
> Justice is the measure of his words.
> He shall not be moved for ever.[2]

And it is thy soul that must be lent as a refuge for their sorrows, thy heart that must be offered as a counterpoise to their doubts, their coldness and their sins, and to love them 'unto the end'. Thou must renounce even the *joy* of loving until the day break, the stone be rolled from the tomb and thy joy rise again beyond death when the Blessed Virgin, My mother and thine, shall look upon thee.

> The flowers have appeared on earth,
> The time is come to prune the vines.
> The voice of the turtledove
> Is heard in our land.
> Arise, my Friend,
> Arise, most beautiful one,
> And come.[3]

[1] Former Mass of the Sacred Heart. Miserebitur.
[2] St. Jerome Aemilian, July 20.
[3] Apparition of Our Lady Immaculate, February 11.

Under the Spirit's mystic touch the Gradual has led us through the unfolding of its texts on the translucent wings of The Cantilena to the ineffable Presence towards which everything aspires. Arise and come.

THE ALLELUIA

THE anonymous Englishman who wrote the *Cloud of Unknowing* puts the following question into the mouth of the disciple he is guiding to contemplation. 'Now thou askest me and sayest: How shall I think on God, and what is He? Unto this I cannot answer Thee except to say I know not.'

This is the traditional teaching of all the great mystics. They do not know. Words seem to them a mockery, concepts a prison, the entire apparatus of speech the shadow of a shade.

We were obliged, it is true, to start from language, to push off from the beach with our oar, turning our back to the open sea. We were compelled to utter in words full of earthly associations the supreme secrets of the Divine Life. Faith, it is true, had infused into language a new life and had, by employing the marvellous resources of analogy, expanded without limit the perspectives it is capable of disclosing.[1]

But every comparison was finally compelled to deny itself. For no perfection is ever realised in its purity within the sphere of our present experience, and this freedom from all alloy is precisely the distinctive feature which must characterise God's perfections.

The Godhead in effect cannot be distinguished as one

[1] The capacity proper to those concepts termed transcendental, i.e. above every category and division of reality, to signify similar relationships on different levels of reality.

being among others or as a being at the head of other beings, in an ascending series of which it is the highest degree. It must be distinguished as the Being absolutely transcending not only each created being taken separately but their entire series. However far we carry the excellence of the creature it is always infinitely remote from God. To find God we must leave the series to which we are too inclined to imagine that He belongs and seeking, so to speak, to 'undefine' rather than to define Him, realise that we begin to know Him truly in so far as we recognise that He is infinitely above every concept, as He is above every word, and that the name which fits Him better than any other is the *ineffable*, because it is content to call Him '*He that cannot be uttered*'. 'Thou art a God ineffable, incomprehensible, invisible and beyond our grasp'; as it is finely expressed in the Liturgy of St. John Chrysostom. From this point of view, few pages give such delight to the believer, Denys excepted,[1] as the article in his Summa which St. Thomas devotes to the relation between the sixth beatitude and the gift of understanding, where he speaks of this vision, in which 'though we do not see what God is, at least we see *what he is not*', and adds that 'the more perfectly we know God in this life, the more we understand that He exceeds whatever the intellect can understand'.[2] This *denial*, however, is the supreme *affirmation* of our understanding. For it is the refusal to limit the Infinite. And the heart has the wider field for its love, and feels itself free at last to attach itself fully without being made captive. Impatient now of the oars which beat the waves to the laborious rhythm of

[1] The Pseudo-Denys. On the Divine Names, Mystical Theology and the Celestial Hierarchy. Trad. Darboy. p. 10, 159, 164–5.
[2] 2a, 2ae IX. 7, c.

thought, it asks that the sail be hoisted and that it be permitted to follow freely the wind of the Spirit through ' the Cloud of Unknowing' to the silent abyss of love where every being has its birth.

God's incomprehensible transcendence, far from banishing Him to an inaccessible sublimity, assures us that His relations with the universe are infinitely gratuitous and that no other bond with His creatures is possible than His goodness which diffuses itself and His love which gives. What could He expect or receive who is the fullness of being ? He truly gives what He gives, He gives even what He asks, He gives twice what He receives.

Therefore, inasmuch as the Ineffable Love is His Name, ' He that cannot be uttered' cannot be subject to any necessity in His dealings with us. Our dependence upon Him gives us being ; it does not enrich Him.

If He makes us the object of His power, it is, therefore, always in order to make us the object of His love. In our regard He is all heart, He is a mother. And since we have no hold upon being except His will, always in action, to give it us, we are born every moment, of His love. The sublimest theology issues without denying itself, as it is deepened by the light of infused wisdom, in the tenderest filial charity.

No longer able to hold back its rapture, and having moreover climbed above the zone of words, the jubilant soul bursts into the ecstatic vocalisations[1] of the Alleluia. ' He who jubilates,' St. Augustine explains, ' utters no words, but a sound of joy without words : for it is the voice of the spirit lost in joy, expressing that joy to the utmost of its power but unable to define its meaning.'[2]

---

[1] Development of the melody on a single vowel.　　[2] On Ps. xc. 4.

' And who is the fit object of this jubilation but the ineffable God ? Ineffable indeed is He whom thou canst not name. But if thou canst not name Him, yet may not keep silence, what canst thou do but jubilate, that thy heart may rejoice without words, and the immensity of thy joy escape the constraint of syllables.'[1]

It would be impossible to express better the mystery of the Alleluia, its sublime aspiration to utter the *ineffable* by the ineffable.

A verse has, it is true, been added to the Alleluia by which the supple inflections of its vocalisation continue their luminous jubilee. But the principle remains inviolate. For it is through the porch of the Ineffable that we enter this garden where all the harmonies of nature, all the delights of colour, scent and rhythm, all the mystic cadences of prayer, blend in a virginal choir to welcome ' fair Love ', at His mother's silent visit.

> Alleluia, Alleluia !
> Come our Queen, come our Lady
> Into thy garden,
> The scent of thy garments
> Is sweeter than incense.[2]

[1] On Ps. xxxii, 1, 8. Texts quoted by A. Gastoué : *Les origines du chant romain*, p. 26.

[2] Our Lady, Queen of All Saints and Mother of Fair Love. May 21 for some places.

THE SEQUENCE

WHEN the Alleluia, having soared to its highest point, bends earthward once more to return to vocal chant, a rocket, as it were, dissolves into sparkling stars, the neums spread out into a shower and give rise to the Sequence.[1]

VICTIMAE PASCHALI LAUDES

The holy paschal work is wrought,
　　The victim's praise be told :
The loving shepherd back hath brought
　　The sheep into his fold ;
The just and innocent was slain
　　To reconcile to God again.

Death, from the Lord of life hath fled—
　　The conflict strange is o'er ;
Behold! he liveth that was dead,
　　And lives for evermore ;
Mary, thou soughtest him that day ;
　　Tell what thou sawest in the way.

I saw the empty cavern's gloom,
　　I heard the angel's story :
I saw the garments in the tomb,
　　I saw his risen glory.

[1] The Sequence, according to the usual explanation, originated in an attempt to fit words to the vocalisation of the Alleluia which was considered too lengthy. This, however, is not true of the Sequences which survive in the present Roman Missal.

Christ, my hope, arises : he
  'Fore you goes to Galilee.
We know that Christ hath pierced the grave :
  Then, Victor King, thy people save!

                 Amen. Alleluia.

LAUDA SION

Sing forth, O Sion, sweetly sing
The praises of thy shepherd king,
  In hymns and canticles divine :
Dare all thou canst, thou hast no song
Worthy his praises to prolong,
  So far surpassing powers like thine.

To-day no theme of common praise
Forms the sweet burden of thy lays—
  The living, life-dispensing food—
That food which at the sacred board,
Unto the brethren twelve, our Lord
  His parting legacy bestowed.

Then be the anthem clear and strong,
Thy fullest note, thy sweetest song,
  The very music of the breast :
For now shines forth the day sublime
That brings remembrance of the time
  When Jesus first his table blest.

Within our new king's banquet-hall,
They meet to keep the festival
  That closed the ancient paschal rite :
The old by the new replaced,
The substance hath the shadow chased
  And rising day dispels the night.

Christ willed what he himself had done
Should be renewed while time should run,
   In memory of his parting hour :
Thus, tutored in his school divine,
We consecrate the bread and wine,
   And lo! a Host of saving power.

This faith to Christian men is given—
Bread is made flesh by words from heaven ;
   Into his blood the wine is turned :
What though it baffles nature's powers
Of sense and sight ? This faith of ours
   Proves more than nature e'er discerns.

Concealed beneath the twofold sign
Meet symbols of the gifts divine,
   There lie the mysteries adored :
The living body is our food :
Our drink the ever precious blood ;
   In each, one undivided Lord.

Not he that eateth it divides
The sacred food which whole abides
   Unbroken still, nor knows decay :
Be one, or be a thousand fed,
They eat alike that living bread
   Which, still received, ne'er wastes away.

The good, the guilty share therein,
With sure increase of grace or sin,
   The ghostly life or ghostly death :
Death to the guilty ; to the good
Immortal life. See how our food
   Man's joy or woe accomplisheth.

We break the sacrament ; but bold
And firm thy faith shall keep its hold ;
Deem not the whole doth more enfold
   Than in the fractured part resides :

Deem not that Christ doth broken lie;
'Tis but the sign that meets the eye;
The hidden deep reality
   In all its fulness still abides.

Behold the bread of angels, sent
The bread for God's true children meant,
For pilgrims in their banishment,
   That may not unto dogs be given:
Oft in the olden types foreshadowed;
In Isaac on the altar bowed,
And in the ancient paschal food,
   And in the manna sent from heaven.

Come then, Good Shepherd, bread divine,
Still show to us thy mercy sign;
Oh! feed us still, still keep us thine;
So may we see thy glories shine
   In fields of immortality:
O thou, the wisest, mightiest, best,
Our present food, our future rest,
Come make us each thy chosen guest,
Co-heirs of thine, and comrades blest.
   With saints whose dwelling is with thee.
              Amen. Alleluia.

VENI SANCTE SPIRITUS

Holy Spirit, come and shine
On our souls with beams divine,
   Issuing from thy radiance bright.

Come, O Father of the poor
Ever bounteous of thy store,
   Come, our hearts' unfailing light.

Come, consoler, kindest, best,
Come our bosom's dearest guest,
    Sweet refreshment, sweet repose.

Rest in labour, coolness sweet,
Tempering the burning heat,
    Truest comfort of our woes.

O divinest light, impart
Unto every faithful heart,
    Plenteous streams from love's bright flood.

But for thy blest Deity,
Nothing pure in man could be :
    Nothing harmless, nothing good.

Wash away each sinful stain,
Gently shed thy gracious rain
    On the dry and fruitless soil.

Heal each wound and bend each will,
Warm our hearts benumbed and chill,
    All our wayward steps control.

Unto all thy faithful just,
Who in thee confide and trust,
    Deign thy sevenfold gift to send.

Grant us virtue's blest increase,
Grant a death of hope and peace,
    Grant the joys that never end.
                        Amen. Alleluia.

STABAT MATER

Plunged in grief the mother stood,
   Weeping where the crimsoned wood
   Held on high her dying son.

Through her soul, whose moaning low,
   Told how grievous was her woe,
   Sorrow like a sword had gone.

Oh! how sad, how sorrow laden,
   Stood the meek and blessed maiden,
   God's true mother undefiled.

Trembling, weeping, whelmed in woes,
   Witnessing the dying throes
   Of her own immortal child.

Who is he who would not weep,
   Could he know what anguish deep,
   Pierced the mother of our Lord?

Who from sorrow could refrain,
   Gazing on that mother's pain,
   Weeping with her son adored?

She beheld the torments sore,
   He for his own people bore,
   Bowed beneath that scourging dread.

She beheld her only-born,
   Death struck, utterly forlorn,
   When his parting spirit fled.

Come, O mother, love's sweet spring,
   Let me share thy sorrowing,
   Let my tears unite with thine.

Let my heart be all on fire,
  Still to seek with fond desire
  Christ, my God, my love divine.

Holy mother, this impart,
  Deeply print upon my heart,
  All the wounds my saviour bore.

Let me share his pains with thee,
  Who so tenderly for me
  Deigned his sacred blood to pour.

Let our tears in mingling tide
  Flow for Jesus crucified,
  Till life cease within my breast.

By the cross to take my station,
  Sharing thy sweet lamentation,
  This is my most fond request.

Holiest of the virgin train,
  Do not thou my prayer disdain ;
  Come and share thy griefs with me.

Let me trace his sufferings o'er ;
  Bear the very death he bore,
  When they nailed him to the tree :

Tell his wounds within my heart,
  In his chalice take my part,
  All for love of thy dear Son.

Wrapt in flames, of love divine,
  Keep me still, O mother mine,
  When the judgement day draws on.

Lord, when these my days are done,
    Let thy mother lead me on
    To the palm of victory.

When this mortal body dies,
    May my soul to heaven uprise,
    Glorified and blest for thee.

                        Amen.

THE TRACT

THE Alleluia was originally the chant of Pascal joy.

Though it has been extended to all Sundays and festivals, it has not been able to prevail against the ancient order of the Lenten liturgy. From Septuagesima, therefore, when the Gradual is followed by another text this is the Tract, one of the oldest chants of the Roman Mass.

It followed the reading of the Epistle at a time when there were usually two lessons before the Gospel, as the Gradual followed, the lesson from the Old Testament, and it fulfilled the same function.

Traces of this arrangement, which, however, is merely probable, survive in certain Lenten Masses, in which, however, both lessons are taken from the Old Testament.

Like the Gradual, the Tract was sung as a solo by a Deacon from the ambo. But unlike the former, it was sung continuously without any refrain sung by the choir. It is from this feature that it has been supposed to derive its name.

Others, however, have regarded the name as a translation of the Greek *Heirmos* :[1] concatenation, succession, series. The term designated a melodic scheme applicable to different texts, somewhat as the psalmtones at present. This explanation is perhaps confirmed by the frequent recurrence of the same motifs. Certainly the melody is less varied, if not always less rich, than that of the Graduals. For it often

[1] Gastoué, *op. cit.*, pp. 60–76.

displays an impressive solemnity which is particularly evident in chants of the second mode.

These characteristics, however, are not peculiar to the Tract. The same melodies may be common both to the Gradual and the Tract.[1]

As is still the case, the text was usually taken from the Psalter.

Save for a few verses, the First Sunday in Lent and Palm Sunday provides examples of the Tract in its original fullness with the further stamp of antiquity due to the employment of the *vetus itala*.[2] In the majority of cases nothing survives except a verse or two, the quintessence of the chant which otherwise we might perhaps have found it difficult to disentangle from its context, the living pearl, whose radiance now shines unhindered.

> *Miserere mihi Domine, quoniam tribulor*
> Have mercy on me, O Lord, for I am afflicted.
> In Thine indignation my sight, my soul and my heart are troubled, my life is consumed with grief, my years spent in groanings, my strength is exhausted by poverty, and my bones are shaken.[3]

It is the inexhaustible theme of human suffering. Infinitely more poignant is the suffering of God.

> *Ego sum vermis et non homo*
> I am a worm and no man,
> the scorn of men and the contempt of the people.
> All they that see me deride me,
> shoot out their lips and shake their heads ;

[1] Gastoué, op. cit., p. 76.
[2] The oldest Latin version of the Bible. Cf. Gastoué, ibid., note 3 ; and D. Johner, *Nouvelle méthode de plain-chant grégorien*, trad. Benoit, Chez Pustet, p. 232.
[3] Mass for the Sick.

> I am poured out like water,
> and all my bones are scattered;
> my heart within my breast melts like wax.[1]

Though mothers may forget (their children) I shall not forget thee.[2] Had not the Father given that promise to His only Son, and could not the Son hope in this hour of total abandonment that the prophecy which rejoiced the Psalmist would be fulfilled?

> *Dextera Domini exaltavit me*
> The right hand of the Lord hath exalted me,
> the right hand of the Lord hath shown His might.
> I shall not die but live,
> and shall sing the works of the Lord.[3]

But must not the grain die before bearing fruit, and the woman in travail endure her pains to the end before she attains the joy of holding in her arms her newborn child?[4]

But love is never greater than in this division of her very self, when she gives her life, that another may receive life. And never did the flaming music of the Song of Songs rise higher from the awestruck earth than in this hour when Christ, forsaken by men, is rejected by His Father.

> *Ego dilecto meo et ad me conversio ejus*
> I am my Beloved's,
> and His heart is turned towards me.
> He has brought me into His wine cellar.
> He hath ordered love within me.

---

[1] Former Masses of the Sacred Heart, *Miseribitur* and *Egredimini*.
[2] Isa. xlix. 15.
[3] Our Lady Health of the Sick.
[4] Cf. John xvi. 21.

Revive me with flowers,
stay me with the scent of pomegranates,
for I am dying of love.[1]

He bows His head. He yields up the ghost and from
His lowered eyelids Peace descends upon the earth. The
Kingdom of God has come.

Notus in Judaea Deus
In Judaea is God known,
His name is great in Israel.
His abode is in peace.
His dwelling in Sion ;
There he brake the power of bows,
the shield, the sword and war.[2]

The remainder of the divine promises can now be
accomplished and Christ enter into His glory

Induit eum Dominus vestimentis salutis
The Lord hath put on the garment of salvation,
the robe of righteousness,
as a bridegroom adorned with his crown.
The crown of sorrow hath burgeoned
into a crown of glory,
a garland of joy.
He hath received the regalia of beauty,
the diadem of splendour.[3]

Thus follow each other these themes that interlace and
harmonise in a marvellous symphony of sorrow and love.
A Boundless Sorrow becomes visible in heaven,

[1] St. Mary Frances of the Five Wounds, October 6 (when used as a Votive
Mass in Lent).
[2] Mass for Peace.
[3] Mass of the Crown of Thorns.

mysteriously triumphant, to guide our march to the Jerusalem that is above, our Mother.

> Like the morning star in the midst of a cloud,
> and as the full moon in her brightness,
> as the sun shining upon the temple of God,
> as the rainbow giving light in the bright clouds,
> as the rose flowering in the days of spring,
> as lilies growing by the brink of the water,
> as the fragrant resin in summer,
> as fire kindled on the hearth,
> as incense burning in the fire. [1]

Thus He appears in glory with his radiant wounds.

> *Quasi stella matutina in medio nebulae*
> Like the morning star in the midst of a cloud.

[1] Eccles. 1. 6–9.

THE GOSPEL

THE Gospel is the good news.

'The Master is here and He calleth thee.'[1]

'Follow me and I will make you fishers of men.'[2]

'Let the dead bury their dead.'[3]

'God is not the God of the dead but of the living.'[4]

'I came that they might have life and have it more abundantly.'[5]

'If you hear my word, you shall be disciples of the truth, and the truth shall make you free.'[6]

'I have told you these things that my joy may be in you and your joy may be perfect.'[7]

Life, liberty, joy, thus Our Saviour sums up His message. Life : all the good things, all the hopes, all the promises all the dreams, all the incalculable possibilities at which our love marvels, still virgin in this little baby which its mother shows us with such pride. Does she in fact need anything else to justify her existence in the eyes of the entire world? Is she not once for all redeemed from her lowliness by this living revelation which relieves her, so gloriously, from the beloved burden whose ineffable mystery she alone knew? Who now could venture to call her useless? She is a mother, she has a child.

'Look what a fine baby!'

---

[1] John xi. 28. [4] Matt. xxii. 32. [6] John viii. 32.
[2] Matt. iv. 19. [5] John x. 10. [7] John xv. 11.
[3] Matt. viii. 22.

She dare not say all she thinks : ' It's the most lovely baby ; there never was a lovelier baby, he is unique.'

It is true ; he is unique. For there is but one Baby.[1]

Life develops, the baby grows up into an alert adolescent in a new world that delights his imagination with dreams of the most delirious triumphs. He can do everything, choose everything, love everything.

' Leave him his illusions,' say those reasonable folk who think illusions are indispensable. ' He will learn by experience, like the rest of the world.'

It is only too true. Unfortunately there are a thousand chances to one that he will arrive one day at that tragic mediocrity which would make us doubt the value of life, if there were no youthful eyes to reflect its inexhaustible novelty.

But it is they who see clearly, all these young men, all these young girls who still believe in the glory of life, who entertain the untroubled confidence that they will accomplish what others have failed to accomplish, and have the boldness to express their love by pledging its eternity.

They will speak of illusions when they have betrayed and thrown away their single chance and refused the call that unremittingly summoned them to a task sufficiently great to demand and satisfy at once all the powers of their being ; or rather, for nothing could be more unfair or more cruel than to blame them for the error and the ignorance of which they are victims, they will speak of illusions when their material needs have plunged them into a world where spiritual values are unknown and the very condition of success is an unswerving pursuit of self-interest.

[1] The Babe of Bethlehem who wishes to be born again in every baby.

Then after a resistance, often heroic, not to be made fools of or merely to gain a livelihood, they will accept the ' inevitable ' compromise and console themselves for their defeat by contemplating in a cradle the immortal hope of life reborn.

Blessed are they for this act of faith which they now make on behalf of another, as once they made it on their own behalf. It is their best self that persists in declaring life a gift of infinite value representing the most glorious and most divine quest, for any man who may one day discover its mysterious reality.

It is this reality which the Gospel sets before us by revealing to us the divine vocation of Life.

We have but to read the Gospel attentively to discover that its essential theme is the spiritual and inward nature of the Kingdom of God.[1] In opposition to the pull of His environment, the inflamed expectations of His people, the enthusiastic suggestions of His disciples, the cunning insinuations of His foes, in opposition to the vast network of shibboleths, ceremonies and ritual practices in which life had been entangled by the tradition of the Doctors, even in opposition to the very genius of the language He spoke, Jesus with a Divine pertinacity made this the centre of His entire teaching.[2] ' The Kingdom of God cometh not with observation. We cannot say of it, " Lo here, lo there." For the Kingdom of God is within us.'[3]

[1] This does not exclude, as we constantly point out, a Sacramental entrance into the Kingdom by the instrumentality of a visible Institution. But the sensible elements are themselves occupied *from within* and so to speak *interiorised* by the Spirit that takes possession of them.

[2] That is to say if the Kingdom of God is indeed the distinctive theme of the Gospel, and if this Kingdom is in the last resort : God *within* us.

[3] Luke xvii. 21. Cf. John iii. 8.

There could be no more formidable defiance of the established authorities than this calm saying which stripped them of all the prestige attached to their learning, fasts and phylacteries.[1] But there could be no greater boon, no greater proof of love. Religion ceased to be the appanage of a single nation, the privilege of a caste, the speciality of a corporation. It was Life, life unconfined, life as a free gift, life in its fullness.

It was the newness of this message that scandalised the people of Nazareth. They could not understand how one of themselves, poor like themselves and clad as they were clad, ' the carpenter, the son of Mary ',[2] could suddenly claim a prophetic mission, the power to work miracles and interpret Scripture.

Jesus had been so like the others. He had apparently stood out so little above those of His own age. He had been, so far as they could see, so perfectly ordinary. And now He would have them believe that God was His Father.

They began to apply to Him the tests to which they were accustomed. They took hold of the surface meaning of sayings which He uttered with an inner meaning, the most interior words ever uttered about God's secrets.

He however could but bear His witness and point out the truth, that the human nature they saw did not belong to itself, that it did nothing of itself, that it was but an act of obedience, a living prayer, a burnt offering continuously being consumed in the fire of the Godhead, that it could not even say I, for its ego was not in itself, because it subsisted in the Word, because it was but the living parable

[1] Bands of parchment bearing a passage of Scripture and worn on the forehead or arm.
[2] Mark vi. 3.

of the eternal Word, because it was so poor in itself that it could contain all the riches of God.

'Blessed are the poor in Spirit, for theirs is the kingdom of Heaven.'[1]

He understood why they could not understand; that it was because they came to Him full of themselves, full of their prejudices and their demands, deafened by all the noisy machinery of their extraverted lives. How could they discover the silent sources of eternal life?

'No man can come to Me, unless my Father who hath sent Me draw Him. Whosoever heareth the Father, and will be taught by Him, cometh to Me.'[2]

For to come to Jesus is to live His life by living His death, is to be henceforward but one being with Him, by that perfect disappropriation of self in which the first Beatitude has its eternal roots.

Mystery of Holy Poverty in the substance of Deity, altruism of the Three Persons, in which the Self is the inexhaustible outpouring of a living relation in which the entire being is given.[3]

Mystery of Jesus' poverty in His sacred humanity, completely dispossessed of self.[4] To be nothing but the 'Sacrament' of the Word, man in a state of pure altruism towards God, as God is pure altruism in Himself, towards us and towards the entire creation.

Mystery of Poverty in the Church when she brings the bread and wine to a perfect disengagement from their

---

[1] Matt. v. 3.
[2] John vi. 44–45.
[3] Cf. Garrigou-Lagrance, *Dieu.* 4th edition, p. 510.
[4] Cf. Charles de Condren in Brémond, *A Literary History of Religious Thought*, Vol. III, p. 320. English trans. : 'Yield yourself to God in the very sacrifice made by Him of Jesus Christ, and to Jesus Christ in His losing Himself in God so that God might be All in Him.'

substance only to make the mighty Pauper invested with their liveries and having but the semblance of an object, the leaven of our disappropriation and the source within our souls of an eternal altruism.

Mystery of Poverty in the Priesthood when man is lost in Jesus who says " I " through his lips.

Mystery of Poverty which consists not in a lean face or in a pauper's clothing, food or lodging—though these privations if *freely* chosen have their uses—but in the transparence of a being stripped of self and diaphanous to God.

Then it no longer matters what you do, but what you are. Then men exchange not only material objects but their souls. Then social divisions begin to lose their rigidity and rank to become human.

The office no longer hides the man. He is seen for what he is, and whatever position he may occupy, is able to give all the wealth of his heart.

In this our emancipation and our liberty consist. This inner wealth is safe from any man's robbery. God himself guards it in His heart. And it is measured by our intimacy with Him, and increases as He grows in us, and we are effaced in Him. For it is by giving place entirely to Him that we become the witnesses, guests and hosts of the Infinite.

Like every spiritual creature, we can fulfil our vocation and return to the Source of our life only by the way by which everything proceeds from God : the disinterested ecstasy[1] of love.

---

[1] The term ecstasy is understood in its etymological sense : to be outside oneself, to have gone out of oneself, by the gift of self, by *pure disinterestedness*. Cf. Denys, *De Div. Nom.*, Ch. 4, quoted by Maritain, *Art et Scolastique*, p. 42 : ' And of God Himself we must say that in a sense He suffers an ecstasy of love because of the abundance of His goodness which makes Him extend to all things a participation of His splendour.'

God is Love indeed, and can never be less than Himself or act otherwise than in accordance with His nature. He cannot, therefore, bring His creation to its true end, its spiritual fulfilment in the perfectly benevolent Kingdom of His love, by imposing by force upon beings endowed with intelligence a consent which is worthless, unless freely given. If He has indeed created *out of* Love—since He cannot create from necessity—He has created *also* for love, unable to do other than infuse into His creatures[1] a being in some sort like His own, which is Charity itself eternally producing its act. To refuse Him our love is, therefore, in a sense to make creation fail.

Nothing less than the moral significance of the universe is concerned in this choice. It was to make consent possible that everything was made ; for the flowering of created freedom in the voluntary choice of a filial love.

The entire universe hangs upon every beat of our hearts with the infinite weight of the love that gave it birth and entrusts it to us, that we may seal the consent given already by created being, as the engagement ring that preludes the eternal marriage.

Creation is finished so far as God's work is concerned, but not as regards our work. Nothing less is asked of us than to become ' God's fellow-workers ' in the work of pure love, that is to make every creature the resting-place of His affection and the monstrance of His Joy.

That is why He never ceases to besiege us with His mysterious visits, and in His Poverty to wait for us, that He may give us the living water of His love, as He waited for the woman of Samaria on the brink of the well at midday.

---

[1] So far as they are capable of it.

She was not aware of her thirst. She did not know the Spring. She was a sinner. But she had not lost all sense of the Divine, though she confined God within the narrow geographical boundaries disputed by men. Nevertheless He waited for her and spoke to her.

The natural symbolism of the water provided a starting-point accessible to her. He awoke its gentle echoes in her soul, taking advantage of her replies and bringing out the spiritual implications of the words she had spoken, that as the result of her own effort the light might kindle and enlighten her from within.

Though with great difficulty she followed Him.

Then He struck the direct blow that forced her into herself, by telling her of her sins. It was precisely the sinking of the plummet required to bring her soul into action.

She sought to get away from this delicate topic.

He accepted her evasion which led to the heart of the problem. And indeed her great misfortune was not to know God, her great sin not to love Him. He showed her God's hidden countenance, and revealed to her the Gospel of the Spirit. As though she had been the greatest of contemplatives, it was to her that He said those conclusive words which can never be surpassed, those words alive with an eternal life, words welling up from the Spring and bright with its Light, the words for which her heart was waiting and in which she recognised immediately the reply that fulfilled her expectation, the words which place an impassable mountain between true religion and all the superstitions which display its colours : ' God is a spirit : and those who worship Him must worship in spirit and it.'

Continuation of the Holy Gospel according to Saint John
Glory be to Thee, O Lord

'He cometh therefore to a city of Samaria called Sychar, near the field which Jacob gave to his son Joseph ; and the spring of Jacob was there. Jesus, therefore, wearied with the journey, sat just as He was by the spring. It was about the sixth hour. There cometh a woman from Samaria to draw water. Jesus saith to her, "Give Me to drink." For His disciples were gone away into the city to buy food. The Samaritan woman therefore saith to Him, " How dost thou, being a Jew, ask drink from me, who am a Samaritan ? " For the Jews do not associate with the Samaritans. Jesus answered and said unto her, " If thou didst know the gift of God, and who He is that saith to thee, ' Give me to drink ', thou wouldst have asked of Him, and He would have given thee living water." She saith, " Thou hast no pail, and the well is deep ; whence then hast thou living water ? Art thou greater than our father Jacob, who gave us this well and drank thereof himself and his sons and his cattle ? " Jesus answered and said to her, " Everyone that drinketh this water shall thirst again ; but whosoever drinketh of the water that I shall give him shall never thirst, but the water that I shall give him shall become in him a fountain of water springing up unto everlasting life." The woman saith to Him, " Sir, give me this water, that I may not thirst, nor come hither to draw." He saith to her, " Go, call thy husband and come hither." The woman answered and said, " I have no husband." Jesus saith to her, " Thou hast said rightly, ' I have no husband,' for thou hast had five husbands, and now he whom thou hast is not thy husband. This hast thou said truly." The woman saith to Him, " Sir, I perceive that thou art a prophet. Our fathers worshipped on this mountain ; yet ye say that the right place for worship is Jerusalem." Jesus saith to her, " Woman, believe me, the hour cometh when neither on this mountain nor at Jerusalem shall ye worship the Father. Ye worship that which ye know not ; we worship that which we know, for salvation is from the Jews." (We observe that this controversial

THE SPLENDOUR OF THE LITURGY

position was legitimate for the past.) "But the hour cometh, and now is, when true worshippers shall worship the Father in spirit and truth. For indeed the Father seeketh such worshippers. God is a spirit; and those who worship him must worship in spirit and truth."[1]

This is the Gospel, a spring of living water, in the inmost heart.

Laus tibi Christe !
Praise be to Thee, O Christ !

[1] A portion of the Gospel for the Friday of the third week of Lent.

5. THE SYMBOL OF FAITH

THE CREDO

THE Deacon incenses the book of the Gospels, the priest kisses it, and acolytes escort it with their tapers. It is the eternal Word to which they do homage under the veil of words, the Person of the Word they salute, His Presence they worship. For Christianity is essentially Christ. It is not so much His teaching as His Person.[1] The texts, therefore, cannot be detached from Him without immediately losing their meaning and their life. The cleverness of the critics, their patience and their integrity have enabled them to achieve, and they have in fact achieved, most valuable results in the *material* study of the books which contain the beliefs of the primitive Church. But without the faith these endowments have not sufficed to admit these critics to the inner life of the texts, and make them grasp the continuous, moving and mysterious radiation of the Presence which is their soul.

That is to say, the Essence of their message will never be revealed save to the vision of the believer who strives to live it, just as the deepest intimacy of a person is accessible solely to the love which places us within him.

Faith is precisely this inward Divine vision, as charity is the inner Divine love of the heart.

No demonstration, no argument, will ever be of any assistance on this highest level, that is to say, unless it

---

[1] *Christus*, 4th edition, p. 992.

proceeds from *within* itself and confines itself to bringing out the implicit content of the faith.

This indeed is what Dogma often does, though it is sometimes condemned as a rationalist superstructure, disfiguring the simplicity of the Gospel. For its critics have looked at dogma with the same fleshy vision[1] with which other more radical critics had viewed its sources, that is the Gospel itself.

Dogma, in fact, whose very name often inspires panic in minds genuinely religious and deeply sincere,[2] is simply the orderly expression of the Christian faith, and the progressively developed statement—as the mind grasps the different aspects of its object—of the implications which in the course of centuries have displayed the mysterious fertility of the primitive deposit. Dogma, that is to say, leaves us *at the heart of the mystery*, and always brings us back to *the same centre, the Person of Jesus*. Of its very nature dogma appears incomprehensible to those who look at it from outside. For it is but the progressively more explicit expression of the most intimate self-confidence that God could make to us.

Thus Jesus was no more than a cranky or dangerous dreamer in the eyes of politicians held captive by appearances. They thought they saw Him, because He was before their eyes: His true Personality was inaccessible to them.

---

[1] No doubt in perfect good faith.

[2] Their fright is perfectly intelligible. For they are no longer at the Centre where everything is made clear. And if we would be truthful we must admit that the *way in which dogma is presented* does not always make it easy to return to the centre. It therefore often happens that, if we rehandle problems from the inside and in language not depreciated by prejudices, it is not difficult to show the spiritual fruitfulness of a doctrine which at first sight seemed without bearing on the life of the soul.

In the same way dogma is a scandal to those who approach it from the outside, grasping only the literal, that is the material meaning of its terms. To the believer it is bread of life. For he approaches it from within, as he would approach a *person*, with the humility of Faith and the reverence of Love, as we receive the confidences of someone we love, hearing beneath each word the beating of his heart.

Dogma is always at bottom Christ. Dogma is a Person. Through all the statements that strive to utter Him, it is to Jesus Himself that the entire being is attached by an inner contemplation, increasingly transparent, and an adherence of the heart ever more intimate. Dogma, in fact, possesses a sort of *sacramental dynamism* which makes it a source of intimate communion with God, as it is also the authentic expression of His inner life. Dogma is a sacrament of light and truth to those who receive it as a Eucharistic Communion, and permit the converging rays in which the Divine light is diffused to lead them to the Source whose splendour they do but refract, as by following the rays of the monstrance the sight is concentrated upon the Presence that shines beneath the veil of the Host.

All the dogmas thus converge in God, of Whom on earth we cannot say what He is. They do not claim to remove the unutterable mystery, but on the contrary to plunge us ever deeper into its life-giving waters.[1]

Truth is everywhere and always inner being seen by an inward vision. The more spiritual therefore a being, the more perfect in consequence is its inwardness, and the more interior accordingly must be the vision that aspires to behold

[1] Cf. the suggestive passage in Père Pinard de la Boulaye's *Jésus, lumière du monde* on the life of dogma in faith, p. 108.

it. And where the most intimate depth of the Godhead is concerned, the vision must be infinitely deepened.

Faith which makes us share God's inner vision, makes us conscious of its depths.

To be sure, its light illuminates our eyes only through the veil of our lowered eyelids. Strictly speaking we have as yet no sight, though a diffused splendour dazzles our eyes. But through the words of revealed doctrine we are aware of the living irradiation of a Presence, and by a mysterious circumincession, in the centre of the soul, all dogmas coalesce in the infinite light of the ineffable Countenance. They do but spell out in human language the unfathomable reality of Divine Love.

And the *Credo*, which summarises them all in the Divinely ordered sequence of its sublime articles, says at bottom but one thing, which is everything : God is love. God is love in the eternal diffusion of His Being, the subsistent altruism that constitutes the Divine Persons.

God is love in the gift of His only Son who has truly taken our human nature, lived our life, conquered our death by His death, and foretold our Resurrection by His own : who lives with the Father as our Brother for ever more, our Intercessor and our Judge. For the Father has given all things into the hands of Him who has been in all points tempted as we are, but without sin.[1]

God is love in His mystical body, the Church, informed by His Spirit, which teaches us the eternal truth under the veil of words and dispenses the Divine Life under the veil of signs whose sacramental efficacy it is the function of baptism to inaugurate by depositing in the soul of the weakest new-born babe, the genuine seed of eternal life, a

[1] John v. 22–23 ; Heb. iv. 15 and vii. 25.

seed which will unfold its blossom only beyond the shadows, figures and symbols amidst which faith still journeys before the dawn.

' For we have known ourselves and have believed the love that God hath had for us ; for God is love.'[1]

It is with this conviction, and in this wholly interior light, that we must sing the verses of this vast poem which is faith's altar of repose and the sacrament of its integrity.

[1] 1 John iv. 16.

THE HYMN OF FAITH

I

THE PRIEST

I believe in one God:

Who is Love.

II

THE WHOLE CHOIR

The Father Almighty, Creator of heaven and earth; and of all Things, Visible and Invisible.

In the Trinity of which the Father is the principle, in the universe of which the Trinity gathered up in the Father is the source; of all things from the sublimest spirits to the lowest corporeal elements. The entire origin of creatures is here intended.[1]

II

THE FIRST CHOIR

And in one Lord Jesus Christ, the only begotten Son of God, begotten of the Father before all worlds [deriving His origin], God from God, Light from Light, true God from true God, begotten not

We now hymn the eternal birth of the Word eternally new-born in the Father's bosom, who in Him knows but His own countenance and impresses it after His pattern on the face of every creature.

[1] These notes must not be regarded as a Summa Theologica in miniature, but rough hints for a modest elevation of the mind and heart—an accompaniment, as it were, to the chant.

made, consubstantial[1] with the Father by Whom all things were made.

III

THE SECOND CHOIR

Who for us men and for our salvation came down from heaven, and was incarnate by the Holy Ghost of the Virgin Mary, and was made Man.

And He was also crucified for us under Pontius Pilate, He suffered and was buried.

'God so loved the world that He gave His only Son, that whosoever believeth in Him should not perish but have everlasting life.' Therefore though being in the condition of God He did not regard His equality with God as a prerogative to be clung to jealously, but He emptied Himself by taking the condition of a slave, becoming like men, and shown by His state to be truly human.
He humbled Himself, becoming obedient even to death, even the death of the Cross.[2]

IV

THE FIRST CHOIR

He rose again the third day from the dead according to the Scriptures, He ascended into heaven, sitteth on the right hand of the Father. From thence He shall come with glory to judge the living and the dead, whose kingdom shall have no end.

'Therefore God hath exalted Him and given Him the name that is above every name, that at the name of JESUS every knee should bow in heaven, on earth, and in hell, and every tongue confess that Jesus Christ is the Lord to the glory of God the Father.'[3]

[1] *Consubstantial :* having the same substance, the same essence, the same nature as the Father.
[2] John iii. 16 and Phil. ii. 6, 8.
[3] Phil. ii. 9–11.

E

V

THE SECOND CHOIR

I believe in the Holy Ghost, the Lord and Giver of life, Who proceedeth from the Father and the Son, Who with the Father and the Son together is worshipped and glorified, Who spake by the Prophets.

We hymn the eternal origin of the Spirit who is the eternal kiss of the Father and the Son, the subsistent Gift of their eternal Charity, whose ecstasy is shed upon us in the entire scheme of our sanctification; of which the Spirit is the source, the Prophets the heralds, Jesus he Mediator, and the Church he mystic tabernacle.

VI

THE FIRST CHOIR

I believe in the one, holy, Catholic and Apostolic Church.

The Church visible like the Host and like the Host ineffable, the Church that is Jesus in the humanity He has espoused; the Church that is a 'person',[1] whose form is delineated by these four 'notes'.

VII

THE SECOND CHOIR

I believe in one Baptism for the remission of sins.

The Church our Mother gives us life in baptism in which our 'old man' is buried and we put on the new man created according to God in righteousness and the holiness of Truth.[2]

VIII

THE FIRST CHOIR

And I look for the Resurrection of the dead.

This divine life, however, is too rich, infinitely too rich to manifest all its fruitfulness on this side of the veil. Death, however, represents nothing final. The flesh consecrated by the seal of the Spirit bears within it a germ of spiritual resurrection that will spring up and blossom on the last day when the order of love will be finally established.

[1] Cf. Clerissac, *Le Mystère de l'Eglise*, ed. Vie Spirituelle, p. 45.
[2] Eph. iv. 24.

IX

BOTH CHOIRS

And the life of the world to come. Amen.

Which God hath prepared for them that love Him,[1] and which is the eternal contemplation of eternal Love.

[1] 1 Cor. ii. 9.

II

LITURGY OF THE SUPPER OR MASS OF THE FAITHFUL

I. ON THE EVE OF HIS PASSION HE TOOK BREAD INTO HIS HOLY AND ADORABLE HANDS

THE OFFERTORY

WE enter upon the liturgy of the supper.

Everything that has gone before was leading up to it. We are seated with the twelve Apostles round the table of which Jesus is at the head.

The Deacon has spread the corporal while the Credo was being sung. He has thus laid the cloth,[1] and prepared the holy winding-sheet. For it is a farewell banquet and the mysterious trysting-place with death.

'Whenever you eat this bread or drink this cup you will show forth the Lord's death until He come.'[2] But has He not told us that this coming will not be delayed? '*Ecce venio cito.*' 'I come quickly.'[3] 'My little children, I will not leave you orphans, I will come to you.'[4] 'And your heart shall rejoice.'[5] 'Yet a little while' (it is true) 'and the world shall see me no more, but you shall see me. Because I live, you shall live also. In that day you shall know that I am in my Father and ye in Me and I in you.'[6]

There is the promise and already the source of *life* in the investiture of His death and the silent joy of His return in the invisible light of faith.

We are at table with Jesus, listening to the words He is speaking to His apostles : 'I tell you the truth, it is good

[1] Bishop Wilmart, *Le génie du Rite Romain*, p. 40.
[2] 1 Cor. xi. 26.
[3] Apoc. xxii. 12.
[4] John xiii. 33 and xiv. 18.
[5] John xvi. 22.
[6] John xiv. 19–20.

that I go away, for if I go not away the Paraclete will not come to you. But if I go away I will send Him unto you.'[1]

His humanity had in fact become a snare to them. The body which hid Him from their soul must be removed from their sight; this body to which, though it was in the highest degree spiritual, their carnal ambitions clung so obstinately.

His body must be revealed to them as the mystic Sacrament of eternal Love. It must be set before them as the Crucified body with which they could renew contact only by the Cross. They must enter into His passion, accept His defeat, and feed upon His shame until they themselves died. Then It would be restored to them, but from within, as the glorified and risen body, the body perfectly spiritual, wholly within the Spirit and which the spirit alone can perceive by the illumination of faith.

It was thus that it was already set before them this evening under the sign which truly communicated it, under the form of bread, in which the visible element affords precisely that support which the senses require, that they may experience after their fashion the reality of the Presence which the Sacrament bestows upon us; yet in which the senses can perceive nothing, unless they have, so to speak, entered into the inwardness of faith. The Sacred Humanity will not be less close to them. It will be with them, in them; but their flesh will have no further part in It, and their ambitions will be annihilated in Its own annihilation.

The Word made flesh will in future be seen only under the appearance of an inanimate object. The Word made

[1] John xvi. 7.

flesh, the eternal Word, will become the silent Word. The Divine Poverty has begun its ultimate denudation.

> *In cruce latebat sola Deitas*
> *At hic latet simul et humanitas.*
> On the Cross the Godhead alone was hidden,
> Here even the Humanity is concealed.

Only the silence of the entire being in the death of self can hear the mysterious cry of this silence. Only the poverty of spirit in which the soul renounces the possession of herself can divine the abysses of wisdom and love contained in this unutterable poverty.

Do we understand at last that action must be born of silence, and abide in silence, and issue in silence, and that its power must be the emanation and the radiation of silence, since its sole aim is to make men capable of hearing the Word that silently reverberates in their souls?

Education, government, instruction, and spiritual direction, how all these would be changed, how efficacious and liberating they would all become if parents, politicians, teachers and priests brought to their task the mysterious effacement of the Host, if their words became silent, and the exercise of their authority had no other purpose than to open the soul to the silence of God.

All speech and reasoning, all eloquence and science, all methods and all psychologies, all slogans and suggestions, are not worth a minute's silence, in which the soul, completely open, yields itself to the embrace of the Spirit.

This is the adorable secret of a visit to the Blessed Sacrament or a visit, possible even more frequently, to the Trinity present in our soul and in the souls of our brethren.

Is not this the first Church to build: the invisible cathedral erected in our hearts to the silent Word?

There is no theology more persuasive than this doctrine which cannot be reduced to formulas, taught by the invisible Doctor of Silence, whose lowered eyes spare our shame so lovingly, and whose generous Poverty clothes our wretchedness with such a redeeming compassion.

> *Adoro te devot latens Deitas*
> Devoutly I adore Thee, hidden Godhead,
> Beloved guest of the soul.

My God, Thou art a secret so delicate that only the purest inwardness of the most intimate love can catch its whisper! Surely the poor should feel at home here, those who have nothing, know nothing, say nothing, are nothing. ' O all ye that thirst, come to the waters; and ye that have no money, make haste, buy and eat, buy without money, purchase without price, wine and milk.'[1] You cannot feel yourselves strangers at the Poor Man's Table.

For it is the Poor Man's Table which is the centre of the Divine Liturgy. On the white cloth there are nothing but the morsel of bread and the drop of wine which the labourer takes with him in his worn basket. ' Give Me your life as it is and I will make it My life as it is.'[2] This is the religion of the Son of Man, and this is His liturgy.

He has laid hold of us at the most material and most elementary point of our bodily life, our need of food.

---

[1] Isa. lv. 1.

[2] *Propter immensam suam dilectionem factus est quod sumus nos, uti nos perficeret quod est ipse.*' (In his measureless love He became what we are to make us what He is.) Irenaeus, *Adv. Haer* V. *praef.* M. G. VII col 120. Quoted by Grandmaison, *Jesus Christ, II* p. 635. Cf. In Vigil, epiph. 4th Lesson : Factus est Deus homo ut homo fieret Deus (God became man that man might become God), (Sermo Sancti Augustini).

And He has taught us to eat holily, to eat divinely, to feed beneath a flimsy wafer upon the immortal King of ages, and in the chalice of His Blood to slake our thirst with the water that springs up unto life eternal.

If the food itself can be transubstantiated, so that its being yields to the mysterious invasion of the Lord, and effaces itself before Him, to become nothing but the receptacle of His presence, what can escape the divinising elevation of His brotherly embrace?

The 'Religion of the common place': so the famous preacher of St. Paul's Cathedral described Christianity. The Christian religion is the religion of everyman, the religion for everyman, the religion of all conditions, all hours, all situations and all forms of honourable labour, the religion of daily life; the religion of little things done with great love, the religion of the Spirit and in Spirit, the interior religion illuminating everything from within, the religion that reveals and bestows life, the religion of liberty and the religion of love, the religion which is the interior possession of all things by the dispossession of self, the religion of the Divine Poverty.

And now let us draw near and give the Divine Pauper a little of our bread and our wine, that He may give them back to us invested with His presence, in a communion of His life with ours. That this wonderful exchange may be completely efficacious, and make us truly enter into Him, let us in spirit place on the paten which the priest is lifting up with a gesture of offering all that we possess and all that we are.

Receive, O Holy Father, Almighty and Everlasting God, this spotless host that I offer unto Thee, my God, living and true, for my sins, my offences, and my countless omissions, and for all those who surround me; also for all faithful Christians, living and departed, that to myself and to them it may be profitable unto salvation and eternal life.

The Father, however, hears us through the Son, identifying us with Him in the one gaze of His eternal love. The drop of water poured into the chalice represents this mystic identification.

O God, who didst wonderfully create the dignity of human nature, and hast more wonderfully redeemed it, grant us by this mysterious union of the water and the wine to partake the Divinity of Him who has deigned to share our humanity; Jesus Christ, thy Son, Our Lord, who liveth and reigneth with Thee in the unity of the Holy Ghost, world without end. Amen.

Here we catch a sublime echo of the *Felix culpa* of the *Exultet*[1] which almost praises the sin that has bestowed on us a Redeemer so holy and so exalted. It is in Him that we are now going to offer up ourselves. Our prayer lays aside the burden of self, and taking a loftier flight in the certainty that it will be heard charges itself with the needs of the entire world to commit them to the Father through the heart of His Son.

We offer Thee, O Lord, the chalice of salvation, beseeching thy mercy that it may rise up in the sight of thy Divine Majesty for our salvation and the salvation of the whole world like the fragrance of a sweet perfume.

---

[1] Sung on Holy Saturday at the blessing of the Pascal Candle: 'Blessed sin that merited to have such and so great a Redeemer.'

The whole world. The Heart of Jesus has no bounds, the heart of the Church no frontiers; they are the same thing.

No more may your heart have any bounds. Come here with your brethren. Come for your brethren. Offer yourself for them that your life may be their offering. Communicate for them that they may communicate in you. Then you shall know the value of your day's work, and that you also are a priest after your fashion, or rather that Jesus is priest in you. You will read in the paper the lot of His brothers who are also yours, the mourning and sorrow of His children who are your children.[1] And all this noise will become silence in your heart, all these tears be shed in your prayer, all these crimes be redeemed by your love. And all these agonies will find a Viaticum in the Host that has made His dwelling in you.

' Lift up thine eyes and look around thee. All these gather themselves together and come to thee, thy sons that have come from afar, and thy daughters rising up by thy side. Behold, thou dost abound, thine heart shall marvel and be enlarged, because the abundance of the sea is converted unto thee, the wealth of the nations,'[2] those countless multitudes who bring you their souls, that you may give them your God.

No vaster field of action could be offered to your love. The privilege of your faith could not be more exalted. Never forget that to be Catholic is to carry the whole world in your heart.

We have alas, too often lost sight of this, though it is

[1] ' In every province and every town I have children in God.' Words of a third-century Martyr. (*Acts of S.S. Carpus, Papylus and Agathonice* 32 in Allard: *Dix leçons sur le Martyre,* 5th edition, p. 76.)
[2] Isa. lx. 4–5.

our mission to bring the world light, joy and peace. And more than any others we are responsible for its woes.

In a humble spirit, and with a contrite heart, may we be received by Thee, O Lord, and may our sacrifice be so offered in Thy sight to-day, that it may be worthy to please Thee.

How our brethren would love Christ, if we had a passionate zeal for His Kingdom, and how they would love the Church, if in our lives she always displayed His countenance so that they could give her no other name than the name of Jesus!

How unworthy we are of Thee, O Lord, and what need we have to be consumed by the fire of Thy Spirit!

Come, Thou Sanctifier, God, Almighty and Everlasting, and bless this sacrifice prepared for the glory of thy Holy Name.

May He come soon, whom we await at His table.[1]

---

[1] Apoc. xxii. 2c.

THE OFFERTORY CHANTS

THE authentic constituents of the Roman Rite are characterised by the most admirable sobriety. We cannot even say that the Roman liturgy keeps guard over itself. It forgets itself. It performs the necessary actions in a pregnant silence, without thinking of the effect they may produce. It does not seek to edify, it prays. And its language is as simple as its attitude, as transparent as its gaze, as reserved as its heart. It knows our needs, and voices them by a modest phrase which throws them open to God and submits them to the measure of the one thing necessary, without ever exceeding what a soul of goodwill is capable of desiring at any moment of her life. It feels neither terror nor rapture, and the most fiery biblical texts issue from its lips with the perfect calm of the purest disinterestedness. It pronounces them in and for God. It knows that He alone exhausts their meaning, as He alone can fulfil them. In fact it rather hears them than pronounces them, careful not to restrict their amplitude by any personal note.

There are those who regard the Roman rite as somewhat dry and cold, lacking in imagination and hostile to symbolism. The charge would be justified if symbolism were necessarily an allegory in words or gesture, whose features must correspond point for point with the invisible outlines of a spiritual reality which it represents.

There is, however, a symbolism more profound than

this, a parallelism which divides the attention, since it leads it along the surface of the mystery before plunging it in its depths. It is the symbolism inherent in reality itself, the *symbolism of being* as it offers glimpses of its Source. Every being throughout the entire universe transcends itself and is bathed in the living atmosphere brilliant with rays emitted by the Presence on which all things depend. Every creature is outlined against this mysterious background of invisible Light, in which the interior of its being is revealed—what it owes to the thought and receives from the love of God. Little by little, as we look attentively, this radiance takes complete possession of it, renders its materiality indescribably transparent, and obliterates its boundaries in the splendour to which its heart gives birth.

The creature is no longer alone; it is sustained by this Countenance always new, yet always the same, which our astonished heart rediscovers every time it listens to the profound music of things. This is the birth of poetry, for poetry is being—perceived in its mystery with all its inner tones and all its links with God.

Not every poet, it is true, knows the nature of the music whose silent strain he hears in everything. But every poet knows that he does not impose it upon the world, and that his part is but to listen to the inexhaustible confidences which objects impart to him, subjecting his soul to their rays and allowing himself to be carried along by the vast rhythm which bears him irresistibly to the ocean of Being. Art is continuously engaged in garnering this rhythm by incorporating its liberating energy into the material which it fashions. That is why the artistic master-piece is the work which presents most directly, most inwardly and most silently this suggestion of infinity that restores its true countenance to the world; it is the work of art worshipping the Beauty which inhabits it, the work of art which listens and opens the spaces of silence within us.

If these criteria are applied to the Liturgy, though we must not fail to take into account the unique character of the Mystery it enacts, requirements to which all else must yield, it will be seen that the Roman Church has achieved an unqualified masterpiece, whenever she has obeyed her own genius. Her symbolism has been the inwardness of gesture, her sense of mystery has been expressed by silence. For she has a temperamental aversion to what is outwardly picturesque, self-conscious rites, words which aim at producing an effect.

The Liturgy offers no spectacle to the eye: it is a prayer that has issued from silence to abide in silence, an action that remains within the mystery which it accomplishes, a work wholly wrought of humility, effacement and love. That is why the Roman rite at least left the Mass the veil of its own mystery and constructed no other 'Holy of Holies', save the silence of the Canon. The people could follow every gesture of the celebrant, who originally faced them, as he still faces them in the oldest basilicas of the Eternal City.

Moreover, until about the eleventh century the faithful themselves offered the bread and wine to be changed into Our Lord's Body and Blood.

'A priestly people,'[1] they were more conscious than we of the fact that they offered the sacrifice together with the priest.[2] For they had access to the altar through the

---

[1] 1 Pet. ii. 9.
[2] The Orate Fratres has preserved this sublime thought: 'Pray, my brethren, that my sacrifice which is also yours may be acceptable to God the Father Almighty.'

fruits of their own labour. It was gifts brought from their homes, materials prepared by their own work, that became for them the mysterious source of a deified life.

The abandonment of this symbolism, due to practical reasons, does not detract from the truth it made visible : all men are priests in virtue of their vocation to be ' Christ ' among their brethren, though it is not for all to perform the sacramental rite which restores to the mystical body the presence of its Head. All are sent as living ciboria into a world hungry for God, to inoculate every creature with the Divine leaven that will make it a ' mystery of faith ' by producing in it, to the extent of its capacity, an emanation of the Triune Life. The symbolism of reality will be fulfilled when the creature, immersed in the Divine Source, dissolved in the splendour of His Countenance, and placed in the interior of His heart, will enter so deeply into His depths that it will be accessible only by the act of faith that adheres to the mystery of the Three Persons : in the light, infused into our dim eyes of the eternal vision which scans ' the depths of God '.[1]

It was this train of thought, attaching our daily life to the life of God Himself, which the *Procession of Offerings* sought to arouse in the souls of the faithful, as it led them all to the Altar, there to exchange their poverty with His.

The Offertory Chants preserve traces of this rite ; and their solemn rhythm and their melody, profound as a song welling up from the heart of reality, continue to accompany the invisible procession of souls bringing their offerings in silence to the altar of God's Heart.

A whole burnt offering for sin Thou wouldst not ; then said I, Behold I am here. At the beginning of the book it is

[1] 1 Cor. ii. 10.

written of Me that I shall do Thy will: My God, I will it, and thy law is in the centre of my heart, alleluia.[1]

As thou dost accept holocausts of rams and bulls or of a thousand fat lambs, so may it be with our sacrifice in Thy sight this day, that it may be found worthy to please Thee: for they who put their trust in Thee shall not be ashamed.[2]

It is good to praise the Lord, and to magnify Thy Name, O Thou Most High.[3]

Bless the Lord, O my soul, and forget not all His favours; and thy youth shall be renewed as the eagle's.[4]

Our soul hath escaped, like the sparrow from the snare of the fowler; the snare is broken and we are delivered.[5]

The souls of the righteous are in the hand of God, and the torment of the wicked shall not touch them. In the sight of fools they seemed to die: but they are in peace, alleluia.[6]

The Angel stood beside the altar with a censer of gold in his hand, and they gave him much incense: and the smoke of the incense ascended before God, alleluia.[7]

Confirm, O God, what Thou hast wrought in us, from thy sanctuary that is in Jerusalem: kings shall make offerings unto Thee, alleluia.[8]

The Lord opened the gates of heaven and rained upon them manna to feed them. He gave them bread from heaven: man ate Angels' food, alleluia.[9]

What is their strength, and what is their beauty, but the wheat of the elect and the wine which makes virgins bud forth?[10]

---

[1] Mass of the Sacred Heart Cogitationes.
[2] Seventh Sunday after Pentecost.
[3] Septuagesima.
[4] Ember Friday in September.
[5] Feast of the Seven Brothers and Saints Rufina and Secunda, July 10.
[6] All Saints.
[7] Dedication of St. Michael, September 29.
[8] Pentecost.
[9] Tuesday after Pentecost.
[10] St. Margaret Mary, October 17.

How great, O Lord, is the abundant sweetness Thou hast reserved for them that fear Thee, alleluia. [1]

Whosoever is a little one, let him come to me, saith Wisdom to the poor in spirit; Come, eat my bread and drink the wine that I have mingled for you, alleluia. [2]

In me is every grace of the way and the truth. In me is every hope of life and youth. I have borne fruit as a rose planted by the brink of the water. [3]

All these texts express the faith, fervour and joy of the holy Liturgy. We may therefore most fittingly apply to it the last of them, the fairest praise which could be rendered to its restrained beauty.

For of the Liturgy may be said what is said of the King's daughter in the sacred epithalamium : *Omnis gloria ejus ab intus*. All her glory is within. [4]

---

[1] Eucharistic Heart of Jesus.
[2] Our Lady, Queen of All Saints and Mother of Fair Love, May 31.
[3] The Rosary.
[4] Ps. xliv. 14.

THE LITURGICAL OFFERING

As we have already seen, the ancient Roman liturgy ordained that the faithful themselves should offer the bread and wine destined to convey the Lord's presence, that they might not be inactive before the altar, as though they were unconcerned with what was happening there.

Moreover, the normal effect of a visible rite is to provoke a corresponding interior movement. According to the mind of the Church, the material offering must therefore be the sign of a spiritual, a symbol of the gift of self in accordance with the intentions of Christ sacrificed.

From a very early period the faithful were accustomed to offer, beside the bread and wine, other gifts in kind, corn, in particular, and grapes. In making this offering the faithful wished to support the priests and provide for the poor. Their simple faith forbade them to separate from Christ those who dispense His grace and those who imitate His suffering. Their sublime faith assured them that it was the destiny of all their offerings to become the flesh and blood of Christ ; whether they served for Holy Communion, the priest's table or the food of the poor. ' He that receiveth you, receiveth Me,'[1] Jesus had said of His Apostles : and for the honour of His humble members, ' What you did unto the least of my brethren, you did it unto Me.'[2]

[1] Matt. x. 40. Cf. x. 1 and xi. 1.   [2] Matt. xxv. 40.

The primitive Christians were aware that these words would judge the world.

After the eleventh century, when unleavened bread had been introduced into the Western Liturgy, the faithful were no longer allowed to bring from their homes the bread they had baked for household use. Offerings threatened to cease. But the Church reminded the faithful that they ought not to appear empty-handed at the Lord's table when He brings to it the infinite riches of His suffering and His love. Gifts in kind were therefore replaced by gifts of money ; an offering to the celebrant to obtain a special part in the fruits of the Sacrifice and a contribution to the parochial expenses : in simpler terms, the stipends for Masses and the collection. There is nothing to be startled at in this. Money is as holy as bread, as labour itself. For it is but the substitute for labour, in the exchanges indispensable to support bodily life. I know the dangers of its employment. But I also know that we must learn not to blame things for faults due only to their abuse by human sin.

Moreover, the Church has sufficient knowledge of human weakness to make what provision she can against the dangers attendant upon this institution. She has forbidden the priest to ask anything beyond the amount fixed by herself and decreed that the stipend offered shall retain his entire available intention. And on the other hand she has forbidden the faithful, if they can afford the full stipend, to give less than this sum, so as not to deprive her ministers of their legitimate support. For there is no blinking the fact : when the method and amount are not fixed, the way is open to bargaining and venality.

The Church knows her children, that they are not all heroes and saints, and that too much cannot be asked of them. To ask what is due, command nothing beyond what is necessary and so to temper every obligation that no man can have any legitimate excuse for disobedience, and then to encourage whatever a generous will can add to what is obligatory; this is the twofold aim of her divine legislation, the marvellous balance of the commandments and the counsels.

The commandment, so to speak, opens on to the counsel; what is demanded suggests and invites what cannot be strictly exacted. And the counsel may be regarded as the flower of the commandment; its most perfect fulfilment. We may compare it to the bed of a beautiful river on which glide, laden with mystic harvests, the tall ships of the theological virtues, Faith, Hope and Charity. Thus the commandment is completed by the counsel and the counsel rests upon the commandment.

The commandment is for all, but the counsel for the more generous. It is perhaps desirable that all should attain the latter. But there could be no more perilous delusion than to impose it on everyone. Let us first keep the commandment. Then we shall be in a position to follow the counsel.

Would you obtain the Church's prayers for your dead? Remember that your offering is not purchase money for the Sacrifice, but the outward expression of your love for those to whom faith binds you, and of your charity towards the celebrant, identified as such with Christ. Do not say: 'This is too much to pay,' or 'How much does it cost?' as though you were buying or selling. And if the strict determination of the stipend offends your sensibility, then give more than the amount prescribed, secretly offering the excess for the benefit of the priest's soul and that Christ, in him, may receive your alms.

THE SECRET[1]

THIS is the prayer which dedicates the offerings, and it was originally the only offertory prayer. To-day it sums up in a few words the theme of oblation, introduced by the presentation of the bread and wine which achieved its full development in the *Suscipe Sancta Trinitas*,[2] which precedes the *Orates Fratres*. It asks God to accept the gifts that lie on the altar, and restore them to us with the increase which He alone can bestow that they may become the source of our life.

This dedication is prefaced by incensing the gifts, a rite which invests them with a silent consecration that is at the same time an act of homage, paid by anticipation to the supreme dignity that will be bestowed upon them. The altar itself shares this honour, as also the priests who surround it, and the faithful who take part in the Liturgy, and all for the sake of the unique Presence that envelops them all.

Thou shalt hide them in the covert of Thy Face against the snares of men,[3] the psalmist declares. But we shall presume to continue: Thou hidest thy countenance beneath their features and dost reveal Thyself in them, as they give themselves to Thee.

---

[1] From *secernere*, 'to set aside, consecrate, bless the offerings'; *secreta. Collecta* and *missa* are words of similar formation. Batiffol, *Leçons sur la Messe*, 8th edition, p. 13.

[2] Actually this prayer is but an amplified secret 'for every day', as Mgr. Batiffol says, op. cit., I, p. 23.

[3] Ps. xxx. 21.

The creature's gift to God is in fact, to the extent of its capacity, also God's gift to the creature and the creature's gift of God. For not only is the creature unable to give anything it has not received, and Divine grace always anticipates and invites the offering which it makes, but the gift it offers to God is simply to open its heart to receive a greater gift from Him. God indeed must always be giving. And He always gives more, as we surrender ourselves with more filial devotion to His action; His power embraces us more intimately, the light He sheds upon us becomes brighter.

The more a creature gives itself to God the more intimate the Divine Presence becomes, the more does He manifest Himself in that creature and communicate Himself through it. Thus the apparent opposition between heaven and earth, God and creatures, is resolved in the mysterious circumincession[1] of love.

It may be well to consider this truth. For here below our eyes can rest only on the face of creatures. It is they indeed whom we meet at every turn. To forbid us to see them would be to forbid us to live. Moreover it is they to whom we owe our first revelation of God. For ' from the creation of the world His invisible perfections are visible to the mind in His works.'[2]

We cannot deny this order and pretend that we love God whom we do not see, when we do not love our brethren whom we do see.[3]

[1] The term denotes in the language of theology the reciprocal inhabitation of the Divine Persons. It may be extended to denote the mutual intimacy which renders souls, as it were, interior to each other in the communion of saints, which can be truly designated the circumincession of souls : ' That all may be one in us as Thou and I are one ' (John xvii. 21–22).

[2] Rom. i. 20.

[3] I John iv. 20.

And even if we could love God to the exclusion of the Universe, would not this amount to condemning His entire creative action *and the very being we owe to Him*, not loving the things He loves, the things whose sole ground of existence is His love?

On the contrary, the attitude most respectful of His designs is surely to behold in the immense variety of the spectacle which surrounds us the marvellous reflection of the inexhaustible riches of His Being and of His eternal novelty. For the Christian, therefore, detachment from earth means emancipation from self and opening the soul to all by opening it to God who appears mysteriously in the very heart of creatures to reveal to us, silently in His Heart, the secret of their being. To detach ourselves from creatures is in truth to break down the barriers of self, to uncover one's inner being and begin to love, hearing in everything divine echoes, desiring that all things may be transparent to the light of their Source, and constantly bringing them back to the Presence which alone can fill their capacity.

This does not mean that we shall bestow upon them an undistinguishing affection extended to all in equal measure in virtue of the immutable attribute of existence common to all alike. It is not in this way that God loves them. For it is to Him that every being owes that which differentiates it from the rest, and each is thus the object of a unique love. To love *in* God is to love *in the same way* by willing the entire reality of the gift He makes with all the marvellous unfolding to which it is destined and by always bearing in mind that if God is the Immutability—the infinitely active Immutability—of Life which possesses its fullness eternally, our knowledge of Him must, on the contrary, be continually deepened and renew its ardour at every trace of His steps.

To love in the same way as God is thus to watch like a mother the birth of the ray which in the mirror of the creature reflects the splendour of the Creator. It is to identify oneself with that which in every creature is most mysterious, enter into what is most intimate in it, grow with its growth and expand with its freedom. It is to throw the soul open in company with it to the mysterious demands of Love. For love is seeking to reveal in it a feature hitherto unperceived of that Countenance whose light cannot indeed be expressed by our shade but whose smile can, nevertheless, enlighten our night with a joy brighter than the brightness of dawn.

Creatures then pass one by one through our fingers, endowed by our inner vision with a spiritual touch. They become an unending rosary in which every creature passes through the soul like a prayer. At every step prayer finds a new altar of repose, and the heart can no longer escape its God.

No doubt it is not given to every man to attain the lucid calm which distils from the Canticle of the Sun. To discover its wellspring we must climb Alvernia. We must be wholly crucified to self, to break forth in the hour of this death into ' the praise of the creatures '.

But it is certainly this Vision of the Universe which the Liturgy seeks to awake in us when it prepares for the invisible meeting with our Lord beneath the visible emblems which the Secret now dedicates to the Father who gives us His Only Son to awake in us the liberty of sons.[1] For to be free is to move in God, in Love's boundless spaces,

[1] Cf. Rom. viii. 21.

to move with a motion which is most interior, because we are attached to that aspect of the Universe in which it derives from Being and bears witness to the Spirit. But, as we know only too well, the Universe has another aspect in which it derives from nothing and by which it can draw us to nothing if we keep our eyes in the dark and our hearts closed against Love—no longer aware of the infinite save in an access of giddiness. But to surrender to this aspect is to lose the Universe as much as ourselves. Its secret also is interior, and its true being invisible. Our hands will never be able to grasp its mystery.

Only by raising it aloft in our hearts as an offering, by opening ourselves along with it to the life-giving invasion of the Source, by hearing in it the echo of the eternal Word, shall we attain its essence. All realities will sing, nothing else will, as Coventry Patmore observed.

Faith teaches us what divine amplitude this music can attain when He who is the ineffable Song of the Father sings in silence beneath the veil of the Host.

No doubt Divine Omnipotence alone can thus communicate to inanimate objects the subsistent ' Art '[1] of the Father and His eternal poetry. This is the goal, wholly unforeseeable and absolutely supernatural, of the movement which impels every creature to bear witness to creative Love, as soon as it is awake to its own mystery.[2]

[1] That is to say, the Word who is the eternal exemplar, the archetype in accordance with which all things have been made. Cf. St. Thomas 3a p.q. q. IIIa 8. The designation ' the art of Almighty God ' is applied to the Word by St. Augustine : ' *De Doctrina Christiana*,' l. 5, quoted by Maritain, *Art et Scholastique*, pp. 51 and 269.

[2] ' Dig within thyself,' said Marcus Aurelius, ' within thee is the source of good always ready to spring forth, if thou wilt always dig.' *Thoughts*, VII, 59.

Nevertheless this intuition of the origin and spiritual vocation of being prepares us in some sort for this Meeting which no word can describe, and the sacramental life, in return, normally develops in us, beside the communion with God which is its direct effect, an intimacy that grows ever purer and more ardent with every creature.

All things are yours. But ye are yourselves Christ's, and Christ is God's.[1]

What joy could be greater than thus to be able in very truth to unite every creature to the Father by the Son in our souls ?

We should leave the Secret all this fullness of meaning, for we shall thus learn the joy of *offering*, with hands which in the mystic Lavabo have washed off their defiling selves, and are identified with those blessed Hands that can but give.

May these hallowed gifts,[2] O Lord, make us return, cleansed by a mighty power, purer to their Origin.[3]

This surely is the return of which we have been speaking through the aperture of sanctified matter.

The easy passage from the material to the spiritual, under the conduct of the sacramental principle, is particularly sensible in the following Secret, charged, however, with tragic associations, since it is reserved for times of famine.

[1] 1 Cor. iii. 23.
[2] It is not always easy to decide whether in these secrets the ' gifts ' or ' offerings ' are to be understood as simply the bread and wine offered to God as the material of the Sacrifice, or if they refer by anticipation to the consecrated bread and wine. It would seem that the words are to be taken sometimes in the one, sometimes in the other sense.
[3] First Sunday in Advent.

O God, by whom the twofold nature of man is supported by the nourishment and renewed by the sacramental power of the gifts we now offer; grant, we beseech Thee, that their sustenance may never be wanting to our bodies or our souls.[1]

Another and a better-known Secret dwells on the lowly nature of the starting point.

O Lord our God, who hast ordained that in preference to all others those things which thou hast made to help our weakness shall also be offered to the honour of Thy Name, grant, we beseech Thee, that they may be the support of our present life and the sacrament of eternity.[2]

And it is by giving us *Eternity* itself that they will prepare in us the eternal advent, when they have been invested with the omnipotent efficacy of the Word of God.

May our offerings, O Lord, we beseech Thee, suit with the mysteries of to-day's Birth, and may they ever bring us peace; that even as He, though born as man, shone forth very God, this earthly substance may in like manner bestow on us what is Divine.[3]

Thus in the very flux of our earthly condition we can recover the life-giving stability of the Presence that creates it, and lead, even here below, a heavenly life.

May the offering consecrated to Thy Name purify us, O Lord, and make us live every day a more heavenly life.[4]

[1] Among Prayers for Special Occasions, 14.
[2] Thursday in Passion Week.
[3] Christmas. Mass at Dawn.
[4] Sunday within the Octave of Corpus Christi.

F

We shall then attain the inner freedom which our selfishness has so often lost, but which the Divine Grace which is its source can always restore.

Break, O Lord, the bonds of our sins, and that we may in perfect freedom and with a pure heart offer Thee the sacrifice of praise, restore what Thou gavest before (our sin), and by Thy pardon save those whom Thou hast willed to save by grace (preventing sin).[1]

We have, it is true, the fearful power to render ineffective this redeeming intervention of mercy. The failures of our free will are innumerable. But the resources of Divine Love infinitely exceed its capacity to go wrong, and are always able to bring it back to its native dignity by the gentle violence which Love alone can exert in our inmost heart.

May our offering, we beseech Thee, find favour in Thy sight, O Lord, and do Thou in Thy mercy compel even our rebellious wills to serve Thee.[2]

To serve God is to love Him above everything and everything for His sake.

Mercifully accept these offerings, we beseech Thee, O Lord, by the merits of Saint John, the faithful confessor of Thy name, and grant that loving Thee above all things and all men for Thy sake we may please Thee in heart and deed.[3]

It is in this that perfect joy consists, which no man can impair, for our heart is inviolable so long as it abides in Thine.

[1] To ask the Gift of Continence. Prayers for Special Occasions, 26.
[2] Fourth Sunday after Pentecost.
[3] St. John of Kenty, October 20.

Accept, we beseech Thee, O Lord, the gifts of Thy rejoicing Church, and bestow upon her to whom Thou hast given the motive for such jubilee, the fruit of an unfailing joy.[1]

Joy. Is not this the last word of the man who has met God in the dead of night?

‘ Joy, joy, joy, tears of joy’[2]

[1] Low Sunday.   [2] Pascal’s Memorial.

2. AND RAISING HIS EYES TO THEE HIS ALMIGHTY FATHER AND GIVING THANKS

THE PREFACE

What hast thou that thou hast not received ? And if thou hast received it, why dost thou boast as though thou hadst not received it.[1]

THERE are few words endowed with such liberating power as this observation made by St. Paul to the rebels[2] at Corinth. All that we have and all that we are is a *gift*.

Pride which seeks to claim anything of this wealth as its own is therefore a denial of being. For in effect it denies what we really are and to the utmost of its power divides us from the Source. Could it complete its work in us we should cease to exist. Happily we do not possess the power to adulterate the purity of the Source. God always remains infinitely more the Love that gives than we can be the pride that refuses. And when we confront Him with our *no* we borrow the very power to utter our refusal from the *yes* which gives us being. Certainly there cannot be a more monstrous aberration ; but what a revelation it is all the same of the Giver's magnanimity, and what a glimpse of the mystery of His being. Faith informs us of the ineffable tension in which God eternally issues forth in the triple ecstasy of a subsistent altruism.[3] Being and gift are one in the source. *Being is gift*. The

---

[1] i Cor. iv. 7.
[2] Those in revolt against his authority.
[3] *Ecstasy :* going forth, transport, effusion ; *altruism :* the direction or inclination of one being towards another ; *subsistent :* possessing itself in and by itself, that which constitutes a person.

Father gives Himself to the Son, who gives Himself to the Father in the living thanksgiving in which their mutual love overflows in a new Gift, the Holy Ghost, who is their eternal charity. Nothing is simpler and more detached from self, nothing more disinterested—and that in a sense which excludes all abjection and retains only the surrender to another which humility requires ; nothing is humbler[1] than the personal life of the Godhead in the completely altruistic appropriation of His Being's infinite riches. Self-satisfaction is wholly excluded where the Self is a pure relation, and refers to another all that is its own ; and this vision can never lose the infinite transparence in which the entire Being gives itself.

From this Summit we can perceive more clearly how blind, wretched and ruinous a thing is pride. It reveals the utmost dissolution of a being, its obscuration and barrenness. It is to be in a state of death.

God knows, however, it is not our intention to praise all the fashions of speech affected by those who, often with the best intentions, are so eager to tell us they are nothing. True humility is ignorant even of its own nature. It effaces itself in God, rejoicing that He is all that He is. It no longer dwells in itself, and finally no longer knows

---

[1] 'Est ibi aliud inflammans animam ad amandum Deum, scilicet divina humilitas. Nam Deus omnipotens singulis Angelis sanctisque animabus in tantum se subjecit, quasi sit servus emptitius singulorum, quilibet vero ipsorum sit Deus suus. Ad hoc insinuandum transiens ministrabit illis dicens in Ps. lxxxi : Ego dixi Dii estis. Haec autem humilitas causatur ex multitudine bonitatis et divinae nobilitatis, sicut arbor ex multitudine fructuum inclinatur.' *Opusculum de Beatitudine* attributed to St. Thomas, quoted in Maritain *Art et Scholastique*, p. 245. 'And there is another thing which inflames the soul with love of God, namely the Divine Humility. Almighty God indeed submits Himself so far to every Angel and Saint that he might be thought the purchased slave of each, and each His God. To intimate this humility He will serve them as He passes by, saying, Ye are Gods. The cause of this humility is the fullness of God's goodness and nobility, as a tree bends beneath the abundance of its fruit.' It is in the same sense that we speak of God's poverty.

what is passing there, so completely is its vision directed forwards with no other care than not to sully the light which pours into her. Humility is being ; as it is in truth being with an undistorted perception of its nature and recognising the relation to another comprised in its very essence ; being that is open, in the perfect purity of its unchecked aspiration. We cannot in fact conceive the world as not in one fashion or another in the image of its Maker, and not manifesting in some measure those altruistic propensities so splendidly realised in its Source. Therefore as it becomes intellectually self-conscious as man is in fact, it cannot lawfully will its own existence, save as a gift.

Moreover, since creation springs from the Divine will, willing it with the unlimited gratuity of an absolutely free Gift, thanksgiving should be the first fruits of our self-knowledge, *thanks* the first cry of our hearts.

Here, as on all the paths of light along which his Love leads us, Christ goes before. Thanksgiving was the heart of His prayer, and it was in the form of a thanksgiving that He instituted the memorial of His passion. We call it in fact the *Eucharist*, which means thanksgiving.

He was about to die that indescribable death which comes from within in which the soul is wounded and crushed in the most secret recesses of her being, even before the body can feel its wounds. He was about to die this death unique in its terrible suffering, in which the mysterious death of the soul crucified by the great anathema and the crushing Absence hastened the death throes of the body hanging on the Cross, and delivered it to the visible death that was but a shadow of itself. This was the death He was about to die, and He began by giving thanks for all the gifts which had made it possible, for all the love it expressed, for all the fruitfulness promised to it.

Thus He became our Thanksgiving, and every Mass sends up by His Heart an infinite thanksgiving of redeemed Creation.

> Hearts aloft.
> We have lifted them up to the Lord.
> Let us give thanks to the Lord, our God.
> It is meet and right.

It is truly meet and right, just and salutary, to give Thee thanks at all times, and in all places, holy Lord, Father almighty, everlasting God who with Thine Only Son and the Holy Ghost art one God, and one Lord : not in the singularity of one Person but in the Trinity of one Substance. For what by Thy revelation we believe of Thy Glory, we believe also of Thy Son and the Holy Spirit without the least shadow of distinction. Wherefore confessing the true and eternal Godhead, we adore distinction of persons, unity of essence, equal majesty : which the Angels praise, and the Archangels, the Cherubim also and the Seraphim who cease not daily to cry out with one voice : Holy, Holy, Holy, Lord God of Sabaoth.

What, however, is holiness but the transparence of Being when it is pure donation ? Such a donation constitutes an unfailing harmony in the heart of the Trinity by the eternal and infinite communication of the same being and life.

And since we approach God only by identifying ourselves in some fashion with Him, and sharing His Being and Life, we are called to enter ourselves into this inexpressible harmony, in which men are revealed as within each other in the Unity of The Source, and give each other Peace in giving each other God.

This Community in the Divine Life is the Kingdom of God whose sublime vision is evoked by the Preface for the feast of Christ the King.

It is truly meet and right, just and salutary to give Thee thanks at all times and in all places, holy Lord, Father almighty, everlasting God, who hast anointed with the oil of gladness thine Only Son, Our Lord Jesus Christ, the everlasting priest and King of the universe that by offering Himself on the altar of the Cross, an unspotted sacrifice and peace-offering, He might accomplish the mystery of man's redemption, and having subjected every creature to His sway might deliver up to Thine unbounded Majesty an eternal and universal kingdom, a kingdom of truth and life, a kingdom of holiness and grace, a kingdom of justice, love and peace.

To reach this Kingdom, it is true, we must often traverse gulfs of loneliness and rivers of tears and enter silently the valley of the shadow of death where, one after the other, all the beloved faces fade. For it was founded on the Cross, and Eternity is its span, and the fleshly heart tortured by the former is conscious of the second as a further agony. When shall the lacerated creature be able to clasp in its arms a world proportionate to itself?

Must we always surpass ourselves, always strain towards the unseen, with eyes that are hungry for clear vision, hands made to grasp, always to postpone till tomorrow to-day's hope, always let go those faces that banish fear with the light of their eyes? Oh, how grateful we should be for a moderate happiness could we but keep it, could it be secured against the accidents of destiny and the onslaught of death.

But are we not deceived by a semblance? What do we know of being, save that its value lies in being open and that when it is closed it is worthless? What was it that beguiled us in those looks so frankly turned towards us? Was it not that after a fashion they made us sensible of the personality of the Infinite—yet without contaminating It by any limitation? And would we now prevent their being consumed by this flame, turn their countenance away from this source and confine them to the monotonous succession of an existence which is petty throughout? Shall we make it a reproach against God that He never wills less than the Infinite for His children?

We believe that He has care of our lives. Can we suppose that He abandons our death to chance? We entrust to Him the lives of our dear ones. Shall we hesitate to entrust their deaths to Him?

' My sons have the same God as myself: He can save them,' was Irenaeus of Sirmium's answer[1] to the governor who sought to dissuade him from martyrdom by appealing to his love for his children.

All the ardent desire he has put into our hearts for the happiness of those who are dear to us must burn far more fiercely in His Heart. How can He fail to watch over those whom He has entrusted to our affection to guide them to Him?

Therefore even in the valley of the shadow of death our faith, assured that His Love has not ceased to guide them, can still hope and sing :

It is truly meet and right, just and salutary, to give Thee thanks at all times and in all places, holy Lord, Father almighty, everlasting God through Christ our Lord, in whom the hope

---

[1] A martyr at the beginning of the fourth century sentenced to death by Probus the Governor of Pannonia. Allard: *Dix leçons sur le Martyre*, 5th edition, p. 230.

of a blessed resurrection hath shone upon us, that they whom the certainty of death saddens may be consoled by the promise of future immortality. For the life of them that believe in Thee, O Lord, is changed, not taken away, and though this earthly dwelling-place is dissolved, they receive an eternal home in heaven. Wherefore with Angels and Archangels, with Thrones and Dominations and all the heavenly host we hymn Thy Glory, saying without end, Holy, Holy, Holy, Lord God of Sabaoth.

No doubt it requires a very strong faith to give thanks at such a moment. Christ's tears at Lazarus's tomb are a Divine excuse for ours. If He was seized with terror at the prospect of His Cross, what more natural than that we should shrink from ours?

But he began His Passion by giving thanks in the mysterious preface of the Supper.

The Church teaches us to do the same in the preface of the Mass. God, whose love is infinite, can never will anything but his children's good. To Him therefore we can always say beforehand, I Thank Thee. Later we shall understand. Even if this will be only after death, it will be soon enough.

THE SANCTUS

IF God is not an idol fashioned in our image, He must be so exalted above every creature, that all ideas drawn from the world of our experience remain always infinitely below His Being. On the other hand, if He is the Creator of the universe and can have found its exemplar only in Himself, He must possess in Himself in some way, though in an inexpressibly higher degree, whatever creation contains of being and life.

We are therefore obliged to interpret the world as a symbol whereby God mysteriously utters Himself, and consequently to attribute to Him some at least of the perfections of which the world presents a sketch.

Many thinkers, and not of low calibre, have shrunk from this conclusion. They have been afraid of compromising the purity of the Divine Being by ascribing any attribute whatever to It. Their attitude may have been inspired by so noble a modesty, and a delicacy so exquisite, that we cannot but sympathise with the lofty motives which have dictated it. Nevertheless, the intellects which adopt this position with such a keen sensibility to the Divine transcendence, fail to perceive that if they attach any significance to the notion of God, they must have escaped from the agnosticism to which they believe themselves confined.

The very reserve they maintain, the abhorrence they feel for anthropomorphic caricatures of Deity are a sufficiently clear proof, that they do attach a meaning to the idea of God and that, besides the very powerful realisation of what He cannot be, they have some intuition of what He must be and therefore of what He is. It is in a particular direction that they situate the reality whose approach they so jealously bar. And if this term reality is not totally meaningless when applied to God, why must they forbid themselves a priori to attribute to Him with the necessary corrections, and without attempting to determine their mode of existence in Him, those purely spiritual perfections which morality demands in ourselves?

The universe is not closed. All the lines of its being are prolonged to infinity and direct our gaze towards the invisible Pole to whose magnetism every being is subject. The world is open in a boundless aspiration towards the Fullness of Being on which its entire process depends. Surely it must present some anticipation of this ineffable Goal which its labour tirelessly pursues. How can its countenance, stretched towards the Light, fail to catch some reflection of It?

That we are attracted, is an undeniable fact, and in the very attraction to which we are subject and in the effects produced by it we can discover to some extent the Focus from which this influence emanates, determine the nature of the Force which attracts us.

If this attraction always involves the loftiest moral demands, and if obedience to it infallibly makes us more open, more generous, larger hearted, and more charitable, why should we not see in these *spiritual qualities* the firmest foundations for whatever knowledge we may attain of the Reality which produces them, attributing them to Him in that supreme degree in which they must be His alone?

And if this Reality cannot be less spiritual or less moral than we—whose moral possibilities it constantly evokes, and whose personal influence it so enormously intensifies as we surrender to It—if indeed It cannot but be infinitely more spiritual and more moral than we, how can It possibly be unaware of the activity which it produces, or not be responsible for it ? It is inconceivable that It should be less charitable than we are, that It does not inspire us with charity towards our brethren, or that It is closed to a world which is open to Itself.

From this point of view it is a most remarkable fact that certain philosophers have been unable to escape the notion of a pyramid, a notion easy for the imagination. God is placed at its apex, the inaccessible summit of the hierarchy of beings, and therefore can have no communication with the lower degrees in which they are ranged. This is too material and too external a view of transcendence. Those who favour it lose sight of the fact that being regularly increases in interiority[1] and moral perfection[2] in proportion to its elevation in the scale of being, and that even in the restricted field of our experience the noblest souls are the best able to cure the faults of their fellowmen without humiliating the guilty or falling themselves.

How can it be maintained that Being in its Divine Source is not as moral as It is perfect, as open to all as It is transcendent of all, and as present to all by Its love as It is present by Its Causality ? How strange that it has

[1] It is also forgotten that there is no question here of elevation and distance in space, but an elevation of quality which does not exclude the most intimate presence.

[2] Moreover, this elevation is accompanied by an increasing moral disinterestedness and a progressively stronger desire to give oneself, a charity more delicate, and an ever wider love.

been possible to forget that the perfection of a spiritual being in the order of being necessarily involves a corresponding moral perfection,[1] and that in God where every requirement of being finds its fulfilment the light of Being must be identical with the fire of Love.

It is difficult, no doubt, to maintain the just balance. At one extreme there is the acosmic monism by which the advaita or non-dualistic school of Vedanta[2] expresses its lofty contemplation of Brahma.[3] At the other extreme there is the unpleasing familiarity of those too naïve souls who think that religion is a very simple matter and fashion their God in the likeness of their desires and imaginations. Christianity, as it is in its essence and as it lives in the Liturgy, has succeeded in reconciling these two aspects of Deity, Being and Love, and combines in its devotion the sense of God's ineffable transcendence with the consciousness of His tenderest Love. It has therefore been able to unite the Sanctus of the Prophet[4] with the Benedictus of the Gospel,[5] Isaiah, overwhelmed by the glory of the Lord, and expecting to die beneath the majesty of that vision, and the little children escorting with their palms the Saviour on His donkey.

Without denying a jot of the Prophet's sublimity, Christianity transforms it by the free and happy trust of childhood. God remains the boundless ocean of Being.

[1] Perfection in the order of being must correspond with perfection in the order of action.

[2] School of mystical theology based on the Veda, the Hindu scriptures.

[3] The Absolute, pure light, too exalted to enter into any contact with the diversity of the universe which, however, is an illusion. See the ontology of the Vedanta by Père Dandoy, p. 25.

[4] Isa. vi. 1–5.

[5] Matt. xxi. 9 and 15. ' Blessed be He that cometh in the name of the Lord. Hosanna in the Highest.' Hosanna is hoši'ah-n'a, Save, I beseech Thee. The acclamation is taken from the Gospel, not from Isaiah.

But He is equally the boundless ocean of Love. And in His abysses of light a heart beats everlastingly, and it is a Mother's heart.

All the love in the hearts of mothers is derived from this Divine Source. How loving then must that Source be!

God is more mother than all mothers, infinitely more: as also He is Father, infinitely.

And this perhaps is the deepest intention of the homage paid to the Blessed Virgin by the Church of her Son; not so much to honour the Mother of our Saviour for the pre-eminent holiness with which she is endowed and the maternal share which is hers in the scheme of redemption —though her person is so intimately dear to us and her tender compassion is so ready to aid, but even more, since everything created, even the highest, is directed towards God as its end, to reveal in her, as in a living sacrament, God's maternal love.

Though our vision is confronted with the Splendour girt with the Seraphs' cry, Holy, Holy, Holy is the Lord, the God of Hosts,[1] Heaven and earth are full of thy glory, the Christian soul remains unaffrighted and flinging herself into these depths raises to God through Mary's heart the cry into which the baby puts all it has and all it is.

[1] In Hebrew: sebha'oth. These hosts are the hosts of creatures, Gen. ii. 1, that is creation itself in the harmonious diversity of the orders which contribute to its unity. Here it must be understood particularly of the angelic choirs.

3. HE BLESSED IT AND HE SAID: THIS IS MY BODY

THE CANON

NOTE ON THE CANON

Liturgiologists are in general agreed that the Canon received its final form under St. Gregory, 590–604. 'The text now in use was already in existence word for word at the beginning of the seventh century. St. Gregory put the final touches to it.'[1] This Pope, we know, made an addition to it, of slight importance however, as Pope St. Leo had done before him (440–461). Pope Symmachus (498–514) probably introduced or remodelled the *Communicantes* and the *Nobis quoque peccatoribus*, perhaps also the *Hanc igitur*, giving the latter, however, a form slightly different from the present.[2] It is also agreed that the Sanctus is not primitive. It is not found in the Roman anaphora drawn up by Hippolytus for the use of his schismatic community between 218 and 235. It was the introduction of the Sanctus which first broke the continuity of the Eucharistic prayer (in Greek anaphora; i.e., elevation, oblation), and was also perhaps partly responsible for the silent recitation of the Canon. If, however, this was the case it must be put down to its credit. Another factor in the development of the Eucharistic liturgy may possibly have been the influence of the 'titular' Masses, the Masses celebrated in the 'titles', that is, the parish churches of Rome, in addition to the solemn Liturgy over which the Pope presided. Perhaps the restricted number of ministers and chanters made the Liturgy seem too short, and the Canon was lengthened, while the lack of solemnity led the celebrant to lower his voice.

In any case it is certain that the *Te igitur* and the *Hanc igitur* and even the *Quam oblationem* are prayers of offering. This fact implies that the Offertory was regarded as insufficient. And this in turn would prove, were it necessary, that the explicit prayers which at present accompany the offering of the Host and Chalice did not yet exist. In fact they are not found in the Missal, not at any rate at High Mass, before the fourteenth century.[3]

These facts are not without interest. The marvel is that from these *disjecta membra* there has resulted by a sort of inner fusion a prayer so pregnant with significance as our Canon. The continuity and vigour of the same life have made it a perfectly harmonious body.

[1] Duchesne, *Origines*, p. 186.
[2] Batiffol, *Leçons sur la Messe*, pp. 226–233.
[3] Batiffol, op. cit., I, p. 21, and Fortescue, op. cit., p. 402.

INTRODUCTION

THE Canon[1] of the Mass guides us silently to the heart of the Mystery. In silence we go to meet Silence. We wait 'until He come'. Our eyes, we know, will not see Him, our hands will not touch Him. God is a Spirit; He remains such even in the Sacred Humanity which gives Him to us.

God is a Secret audible only when self is silent.

The very formulae have a silent character. Their sublimity is their modesty. They possess the lowliness of the bread and wine, and their glory is self-effacement. Different conjectures have been made about their origin and arrangement. It is certain that they are not all composed at the same time and that they were refashioned several times before the pontificate of St. Gregory who left them as we read them to-day. Their unity is internal. None obtrudes itself, none forces itself on our attention, none disturbs the silence. Since the mystery of faith is present, they do not attempt to utter it. All their life is within.

Those who, on the strength of superficial similarities which can always be found between the most dissimilar objects, have compared the Liturgy with the pagan mysteries, have not perhaps sufficiently remarked the complete absence in our formularies of that sacred ' thrill '

[1] Canon : rule, the normative prayer which gives the Holy Liturgy its distinctive character and its unchanging fixity.

with which the mysteries stirred the emotions of their initiates.

The Christian Mystery is of another order. And it is precisely where it clasps that Mystery closest that the Liturgy is most careful not to divert into sensible emotion an attention which should be wholly given to the spiritual disappropriation which the Mystery demands. No word, no rite, can take the place of this initiation into the Cross by the Cross. Silence alone can confront the soul with the crucified Love of her God. The formulae say nothing of this meeting. They bring us to it without mentioning it. Like God they respect the secret of the soul, they preserve the spirit of poverty.

TE IGITUR

We therefore humbly pray and beseech Thee, most merciful Father, through Jesus Christ Thy Son Our Lord, that Thou wouldst accept and bless these gifts, these offerings, these holy and unspotted sacrifices, which we offer Thee in the first place for Thy Holy Catholic Church; deign to grant her peace, to protect, unite and govern her throughout the entire world; together with Thy servant our Pope *N* and our Bishop *N* and all orthodox believers and worshippers of the Catholic and Apostolic faith.

This is the ' common and universal ' prayer,[1] which embraces the entire world in the universal motherhood of the Church. From the unity of its scope no soul is excluded. And no doubt this Eucharistic prayer includes a large number in a unity of life,[2] which makes them to be within, even when they believe themselves or we believe them to be outside. The Mass is for all as God is for all. Those who do not recognise to-day will perhaps recognise to-morrow the face of the Mother whose prayer embraced them even before their birth, and in their turn will enter the visible unity, thus fulfilling one of the most sublimest duties of humanity redeemed and called to become mystically, in accordance with Love's merciful demands, one single person in Jesus.[3]

[1] *Liturgy of St. John Chrysostom* ed. Père D. de Meester. 2nd ed. p. 69.

[2] Since without interruption the Mass is being offered for ' the salvation of the world ', there can be no doubt that it is a most efficacious source of grace for the innumerable multitude of souls of good-will who have not yet been able to meet Christ in His Church.

[3] Gal. iii. 28.

The Pope, together with the Bishops, to each of whom is entrusted a portion of the one flock, is the living sacrament of this unity whose source is Truth and whose soul is Charity. His infallibility, like that of the Bishops taken collectively and in communion with him, secures us from the errors always possible to man to subject us to the sole Word that can claim an unreserved assent.[1] It is so little indeed an usurpation in his own behalf that he himself kneels along with us before the Truth he proclaims, as the priest before the Host he consecrates.

In both cases there is the same submission of the man mysteriously invaded by Him of whom he is but the instrument. ' It is not I, it is He who calls you and speaks to you.'

The Pope is the sacrament of unity, but a living sacrament, a human sacrament, one of ourselves. We pray for the man who bears ' the care of all the churches ', the Father of all souls. We pray for the Bishop who shares this divine care and is more especially our Pastor. We pray for all the faithful who bear together with them the glorious burden of Catholic unity. We pray for all our brethren who as yet are not in that unity but who will perhaps yield themselves to it one day, the more certainly, if they find in our hearts the Church's love, the Church that is our Mother and theirs.

---

[1] The infallibility of the Pope and of the Episcopate in communion with him is thus our guarantee that the adhesion of our faith is yielded only to the Divine Word.

MEMENTO OF THE LIVING

THIS universal care, however, does not lose sight of the closer needs of those particularly confided to us. Every soul is unique and must be attached to God by a personal and an immediate bond. In every case we have to discover this incommunicable gift, and devote to that soul a unique portion of our love to be the refuge of her most personal sufferings.

But how can we who are but human beings have a heart completely open to all and wholly given to each ? Only if by a mysterious exchange God's heart abides in ours to welcome them.

Remember, O Lord, thy servants and handmaids *N* and *N* and all those here present whose faith and devotion are known to Thee ; for whom we offer or who themselves offer this sacrifice of praise to obtain the redemption of their souls, and in hope of their safety and security, and who pay their vows to Thee, the eternal God, living and true.

God will always love them infinitely more than we ourselves. Of His Passion to save them, ours is but a distant image. If they escape us, they cannot fly from Him, for they could not withdraw from His Presence without wrenching themselves from their existence. But His Presence is His Love.

' My God, protect them as the apple of Thine eye, keep them beneath the shadow of Thy wings.'

COMMUNICANTES

'GOD has created beings that they might exist.' But it is impossible to exist without acting. And the higher the being the greater the scope of its action. The entire universe, therefore, is associated with God's action, and collaborates in His work. For we cannot imagine a sphere which escapes His Providence. Nor can we imagine an activity which would not somehow partake of his. To observe this order and respect this hierarchy is therefore simply to recognise the reality of God's gift and the generosity with which He has communicated to every being something of His Fullness.[1]

The Divine illumination which embraces all creatures in proportion to their being, predisposes them, as it were, to become themselves luminous centres, embodying in the concrete the stages of our return to the Divine Source. The Blessed, who in the light of the beatific vision share the intimacy of God's life, will have a pre-eminent share in this saving causality and occupy a privileged position in this sacramental economy which is seen ever more plainly to be the secret of the universe.

Since, however, they act with the complete spontaneity of self-giving Love, we must receive their action by opening our hearts freely to it. This is the meaning of the prayer we address to them, or rather to God, reciting the names of those in whom His Love shone most purely.

---

[1] Pascal, asking himself why God has ordained prayer, replies: 'First: to communicate to His creatures the dignity of causes.' *Pensées*, Br. 513.

In communion with and venerating the memory of the glorious Mary ever a Virgin, mother of our God and Lord Jesus Christ; as also of Thy blessed Apostles and Martyrs Peter and Paul, Andrew, James, John, Philip, Bartholomew, Matthew, Simon and Thaddeus (i.e. Jude), Linus, Cletus, Clement, Xystus, Cornelius, Cyprian, Lawrence, Chrysogonus, John and Paul, Cosmas and Damian, and all Thy Saints, by whose merits and prayers grant that we may be defended in all things by thy protection and aid, through the same ·Christ our Lord. Amen.

The Blessed Virgin is named first whose heart was pierced with the great wound. Her Stabat will not end until all her sons are one with her Son. She receives the agony of our souls, offering us the Cross in a Mother's heart, as the supreme gift of Divine to human poverty.

For it is only to free them from themselves that the Father tolerates the suffering of His children, to open their hearts to the abysses of His Light and Joy.

And the pledge of this supreme love is the Blessed Virgin mercifully interposed like an aureole of tender love between the crown of thorns and our torn brows. After her come the Apostles to take their old places at the supper table, humbly glorying in the Lord's life-giving death, which they now behold in the eternal dawn of the Resurrection.

Paul completes their number: the persecutor by the side of Peter who denied thrice, to attest the victory of love and the fullness of pardon, the efficacy of grace and the plasticity of the soul when it permits itself to be moulded: ' like a sprig of hyssop in the hand of the Lord.'[1]

---

[1] Verlaine's exact words are: ' I who am but a sprig of hyssop in the hand of the Lord.'

In their train five martyr Popes bring the Lamb the tribute of their blood.

Cyprian of Carthage escorts the Church Bride, whose imperishable unity he attests in company with Cornelius, more surely by his death than by his words.

The deacon Laurence bears the Chalice he received from the hands of Xystus to contain the precious Blood for which they will shed their own. Five martyrs bring up the rear. Their heads are crowned with a lovely aureole of golden legend woven by the popular devotion to which they owe their place here.

The list might have been enlarged.

These names suffice, mentioned here as witnesses to the communion of Saints. The Church is *one* in heaven and on earth. The stern of the vessel no doubt is still in the darkness. But the prow advances, shining into the living light of eternal glory. Our stammerings are amplified by the praise of the Saints, and the succour of their loving kindness as it shines upon us calms our trembling hearts. How could they fail to love who are at the heart of love, or to act who possess the fullness of life ? But if they are such loving brothers, it is because God is infinitely more loving : Our Father.

HANC IGITUR

We belong to a family, ' we are of the race of God.'[1] This was suggested by the profound significance of the term communion with which the prayer we have just read opened, and by the care for us which it implied of our elder brothers, the Saints in glory. The prayer we are now to consider contains the actual word ' family ' with all its instructive associations.

A family is, so to speak, one person in several members. To belong to a family is to be embraced by a love which, in a sense, is constantly bringing every member of it to birth. Its members may indeed be engaged in very different occupations and speak very seldom of their most intimate concerns and the value they attach to the home. The home is nevertheless always present as a mysterious atmosphere which they breathe, and there are times when the place it occupies, the many activities it shelters and the different faces meeting there suddenly melt into the silent intimacy of souls. We share something infinitely sweet for which there is no name. We feel ourselves one. We are at the centre. And we suddenly perceive that the active tasks which weave, as they pass, the web of daily life are but the visible projections of this silent bond which is heat and light, welcome and love, spirit and life indescribably bright and so complete that time cannot touch it. The exterior exists only for the interior, and the

[1] Acts xvii. 28.

successive manifold of visible actions is wholly directed to the peaceable performance of the one act, which is life[1] concentrated to the utmost intensity.

This is evident in art. In art the moment of creation is the moment when the material loses its externality, the vision dawns and the sight is freed from time.

How can we fail to perceive that eternity is our fatherland, and the invisible world our home? Like Tobias' Angel we appear to feed on earthly meats when our heart is tasting unseen a heavenly food. For we are marching towards eternal life in the very midst of the vicissitudes of this sensible world, permanently attached, by the most precious gifts that world affords, to the mysterious Presence which sways our highest states and is revealed by faith, as the ineffable family of Three Persons in whose intimacy charity makes us alive.

Since we compose God's family as the prayer affirms, we really belong to it, one family with Him in the invisible home of His Spirit. We could not be more ennobled. That nobility should be our inspiration. ' We are of His race.' Our features should bear its impress, our manners display it.

And this above all is our comfort and our security : that we are God's children. May the priest's outstretched

---

[1] It is a defect of Christian iconography that for the most part it fails to convey the simultaneous fullness of eternal Life—of which the summits of human life afford an image—except by a lifeless rigidity of feature and limb. The result is something so insipid and so unattractive that the violence of a boxing match seems a thousand times richer in content than this colourless eternity. Happily the reality is very different, something whose splendid violence Jesus compared to that of fire. ' I am come to cast fire on earth ' (Luke xii. 49). In this connection we cannot refrain from calling attention to the art, so admirably contemplative and perfectly obedient, of the painter and sculptor, Henri Jacques Masson, who is without doubt one of the artists most capable of bringing to perfection a living work in the silence of the sanctuary.

hands invest the offering with our perfect trust, and this gesture of propitiation[1] be also the sign of our surrender.

We therefore beseech Thee, O Lord, to be appeased and to receive this offering which we, Thy servants and Thy whole family make unto Thee; order our days in Thy peace; grant that we be rescued from eternal damnation and counted within the flock of Thine elect. Through Christ our Lord. Amen.

We belong to a family, have a dwelling of whose door love is the key. However outcast we may be, in God we always possess, if our heart is but open, our home.

[1] Gesture of *propitiation*, which seeks to render propitious, favourable. It is a term often combined with that of sacrifice, and is naturally evoked by the priest's hands extended over the offering, as those of the priest under the old law were extended over the sacrificial victim (Exod. xxix. 10–15). When speaking of the Collect we pointed out the sense we must attach to prayer, and that its object is to bend the inflexibility not of God but of ourselves. ' Jesus prayed for men and was not heard.' Pascal, *Mystère de Jésus*, Br. 553.

QUAM OBLATIONEM

THIS 'home' is ourselves at home in God, though this is possible only if He first is at home in us. The riches of His being must indeed be transfused into us, if we are to become capable of living His life. We must be raised after a fashion to the degree of spirituality and interiority proper to God's life, if that Life is to spring up in us as the supreme expression of our own. This, however, cannot be accomplished without a transformation so profound, that it will appear our death. The bounds of our familiar horizon will recede to infinity, and it will therefore seem to us that we have been permanently banished from our native land.

This, no less, is the cost of our Divine schooling. We must be stripped of ourselves to be reclad with God by a species of moral transubstantiation which makes the Divine Self our own.

This, however, cannot be accomplished, unless we consent to the change with our whole mind, our whole soul, our whole heart and our whole strength. The *Quam oblationem* implores the grace to utter this fiat with a surrender complete, as that with which the Blessed Virgin uttered hers on the day of her Annunciation, when she was offered the motherhood that must bleed even to the foot of the Cross.

Which oblation we beseech Thee, O God, deign to make blessed, enrolled (in the book of life), ratified, spiritual and acceptable, that it may become *for us* the Body and Blood of thy most beloved Son, our Lord Jesus Christ.

The material offering which we dedicated in all the Offertory prayers was clearly but the symbol of this wholly spiritual gift of ourselves which is the essential demand of the Sacrifice in which we are taking part. In any event Christ's assent is pledged, and His word on the priest's lips will infallibly effect what it states. But though really endowed with His presence, the consecrated bread and wine will avail us nothing unless our love assimilates them, *spiritually* making them *for us*[1] what they actually are in themselves : the Body and Blood of our Lord Jesus Christ.

The moment therefore has come to surrender our lives to Jesus that He may dispose of them as He wills, dying to ourselves as He dies for us. May the Divine words which express and effect the gift of His presence also express and effect the gift of ourselves, making us wholly present to Him.

---

[1] Is not this perhaps the meaning of the epiclesis of the Byzantine liturgies though it follows the Consecration, that the bread and wine may become *for us* by the Power of the Holy Ghost, our Lord's Body and Blood ? Cf. *The Liturgy of St. John Chrysostom*, ed. De Meester, p. 144. Ὥστε γενέσθαι τοῖς μεταλαμβάνουσιν εἰς νῆψιν ψύχης κ.τ.α.

THE CONSECRATION

WHO THE DAY BEFORE HE SUFFERED TOOK
BREAD INTO HIS HOLY AND ADORABLE HANDS
(*an expression of the Church's love*) AND WITH EYES
RAISED TO THEE, O GOD, HIS ALMIGHTY FATHER,
GIVING THANKS TO THEE, BLESSED, BROKE, AND
GAVE IT TO HIS DISCIPLES, SAYING: TAKE AND
EAT YE ALL OF THIS FOR:

THIS IS MY BODY

IN LIKE MANNER AFTER HE HAD SUPPED, TAKING
ALSO THIS PRECIOUS CHALICE INTO HIS HOLY
AND ADORABLE HANDS AND GIVING THANKS TO
THEE, HE BLESSED AND GAVE IT TO HIS DISCIPLES,
SAYING: TAKE AND DRINK YE ALL OF THIS FOR:

THIS IS THE CHALICE OF MY BLOOD OF
THE NEW AND ETERNAL TESTAMENT (*the
mystery of faith*) WHICH SHALL BE SHED FOR
YOU AND FOR MANY UNTO THE REMISSION
OF SINS.

AS OFTEN AS YE SHALL DO THESE THINGS,
YE SHALL DO THEM IN REMEMBRANCE OF ME.

'You shall call upon me and I will hear you.'[1] 'I will
not leave you orphans, I will come unto you,'[2] and ' your

---

[1] Jer. xxix. 12.   [2] John xiv. 18.

heart shall rejoice '.[1] '[The Lord] is not the God of the dead but of the living.'[2] The memorial of death is the source of life. The recital of the past fills the present with its Divine Reality. For eternal love clasps all ages in the same maternal embrace in which the beloved Disciple rested at the supper.

'Behold the heart that has so loved men.'[3] God is a heart, God is all heart, God is nothing but a heart. 'God is Love.'[4]

Lord, what hast Thou done and how has Thy Word passed my lips? I obeyed: do the same; I performed the work my Father entrusted to Me. I fed upon His will.[5] Do the same, if you would feed upon Me. 'The words that I have spoken unto you are spirit and life.'[6] And it is spiritually that you must eat my Body and drink my Blood by entering into the supreme Poverty of the eternal holocaust that is Myself: 'The flesh profiteth nothing.'[7]

Our flesh, O Lord, profits nothing; but what of Thine?

My Flesh is the Sacrament of the Spirit. It is but a transparent veil covering the abysses of silence filled by the Word, and you do it wrong if you would understand it by your own flesh.[8] For it is by your spirit that you must attain my flesh; by your immolation that you must assimilate My own; by expropriating yourselves that

---

[1] John xvi. 22.
[2] Matt. xxii. 32.
[3] Revelations of St. Margaret Mary.
[4] 1 John iv. 8.
[5] John iv. 34.
[6] John vi. 64.
[7] John vi. 64.
[8] *Ergo nec Carnem debemus sapere secundum carnem.* Therefore the very Flesh (Christ's) we must not conceive according to the flesh. Eighth Lesson. infra Oct. SSmi Corp. Christi, Sermo S. Augustini, Ep.

you must be incorporated into the living Host of My humanity. Dispossess me, O Lord, of myself, and as your Humanity subsists in the Word that is its Self, so may I myself live in Thee, by Thee and for Thee, depending upon Thee as my true Self, and freed from my selfish and carnal self.[1]

This is what I have always invited you to do. Have I not said by your lips:

This is *My* Blood.
This is *My* Body.

Am not I the priest in you, the sole priest and the sole sacrifice? Have you not understood that your priesthood is to be no longer yourself but I: and to let Me say I through your lips, with your heart, by your life. It was by the washing of feet that I declared the significance of hierarchies: to serve on bended knee, and thus to evoke by the power of humility and love the Father's countenance in the soul even of the traitor and the renegade. In truth there is no state of poverty more substantial than yours. For it is the poverty of Him who has renounced the possession of himself.

[1] Cf. the fine passage from Cardinal Bérulle quoted by Henri Brémond, *A Literary History of Religious Thought in France*, Vol. III, Eng. Tr., p. 71: 'We should regard Jesus as our fulfilment; for He is and wills so to be, since the Word is the fulfilment of the human nature existent in Him. For as this nature, considered in its origin, is in the hands of the Holy Spirit Who drew it from nothingness, stripping it of its subsistence to give it to the Word, that the Word may invest and appropriate it, giving Himself to it, thus fulfilled with His own Divine Subsistence; so are we in the hand of the Holy Spirit Who draws us from sin, uniting us to Jesus, as Spirit of Jesus emanating from Him, acquired and sped forth by Him.' Cf. later, ibid., p. 404, the sublime teaching of Père Condren. 'We should go to Communion in obedience to the desire of Jesus Christ to receive us into Himself, into His life and Being, destroying our own life and being, transforming us into what He is, namely, life, love, truth, virtue for God, and also in obedience to His Will to have us for members, in whom He may live to His Father.'

My God, is it indeed thus? Oh that I may resign myself, may leave the entire place to Thee and become the completely transparent window through which Thy face shines.

Behold my body in exchange for Thine; behold my blood. I offer them to Thee that they may become in Thy hands a living victim in which my brethren may see the light of Thy countenance and divine the beating of Thy heart.

Thus at the climax of the liturgy the mysterious transfer is accomplished; when the church is full of silence, when the words that command substance fall silently from the sacramental lips, when the priest's hands raise aloft the living emblems of the mighty Pauper, when the Host rises above the horizon like another sun, when the Chalice contains the whole of space in a drop of Blood, when the sound of the bell gathers up all voices in the harmonious surge of its waves, a uniform sound beating, like the luminous sound of the stricken anvil, upon the echoing walls of the brass that sings:

The Mystery of Faith.

The life of the world hang on this point.

From the heart opened by that final wound, the hungry Church, to make even old men, infants newborn, receives the Water and the Blood.

UNDE ET MEMORES[1]

WHAT can be said now that will not profane the vastness of the Mystery, and violate the humility of a silence in which God annihilates Himself? The Church has found the language *miraculously* bare into which self cannot intrude at any point.

When the eternal Word is uttered by the lips of sinful man, it would have been so easy to burst out into protestations of unworthiness and evoke the awe of the prophets confronted with the Divine Glory. But since it is God who has willed the condescension, it is far simpler to take refuge in the wisdom of His love. We have remembered Thy command, and we have *obeyed* it in memory of Thee:

Wherefore, O Lord, we Thy servants, and all Thy holy people calling to mind the blessed passion of the same Christ Thy Son, our Lord, also His Resurrection from the dead and His glorious Ascension into heaven, offer unto Thy sublime majesty, of Thine own presents and gifts,[2] a pure victim, a holy victim, a spotless victim, the holy bread of eternal life and the cup of everlasting salvation.

The mystery of sorrow rests upon the glorious mysteries which complete it. For Him at least it is finished. Piety is comforted by the thought that He can suffer no more, save in us, the Passion in which all our sins crucified Him, all our pains weighed upon Him.

[1] This prayer is called the *anamnesis*, recollection.
[2] There is a similar formula in the liturgy of St. John Chrysostom, op. cit., p. 140. Τὰ σὰ ἐκ τῶν σῶν σοὶ προσφέρομεν.

His wounds, however, remain, eternal witnesses, a living prayer, whose infallible efficacy is extended throughout space by the five signs of the Cross which the priest makes over the sacred gifts.

By adhering to the Sacrifice whose impress they retain for ever, we appropriate its virtue. Christ's death is life in us, and His Love fills our hearts with Its fullness. It is He whom our love offers. It is Jesus our gift: We offer Thee, O Father, from Thine own gifts, our gift, which is no less than Thine.

SUPRA QUAE

THE mention in this prayer of the sacrifices of the Old Law, while bringing into relief the excellence of the Sacrifice of the New Law, also envelops all ages in its inexhaustible power. The Cross enfolds them all in its mysterious embrace, and the Divine Martyr's Blood is poured upon them all, a baptism of life.

All ages are Christian in virtue of the hope which fills them, all souls Christian in proportion to their good will.

Even if they do not know Christ it is He, nevertheless whom even their most ignorant desires invoke, and if they are ignorant even of the Saviour's name, He calls them each by name from Calvary's height, the summit of history.

All genuine spiritual life is His gift, all light and all grace derive from His fullness.

Without abandoning the Christian standpoint, the Dies Irae could recognise the Sybil as a prophetess, and Virgil's Fourth Eclogue could pass for an inspired prophecy, so obvious was it to Christian humanists that every intuition of a better future must be a presentiment of His coming ' who is the desire and expectation of the gentiles '.[1]

Christ is the centre of history and of the Universe alike, if it is indeed true that the entire creation awaits deliverance ' from the bondage of corruption to partake the glorious liberty of the children of God '.[2]

[1] Cf. *Virgil*, ed. Lechatellier, p. 21.   [2] Rom. viii. 20–22.

Everything is for Christ, and Christ belongs to all and is for all. The Catholic Faith rejoices that she can give Him to every creature, inviting to *his altar* all who have waited for Him, all who have sought Him, all who have been in their hearts disciples of 'The Unknown God'. Abel approaches with the lamb which was the firstfruits of his flock, Abraham leads his son, like himself Jesus' ancestor, and Melchisedech brings the bread and wine. The Lamb of the eternal Sacrifice will be the Son, and it is under the form of *bread* and *wine* that the virtue of His immolation will always reach, from the rising to the setting sun.

It is not surprising that these figures should assist at our sacrifice. In truth it is not words alone which prophesy but events themselves and the persons who enact them and the material factors involved in them. Everything serves the Spirit 'who fills the earth and hath knowledge of every voice ',[1] and the ' Wisdom that reaches mightily from end to end of the world and disposeth all things sweetly '.[2]

A Creation has not been abandoned to chance. The infinitely various beings it contains compose a universe : a *unity* whose equilibrium is continually being reconstituted by a mysterious solidarity and whose evolution is directed by a single aim, a spiritual aim.

It might seem, it is true, that the history of the universe, so far as we know it, has no relation to mind, which makes its appearance so late and develops so slowly, and with whose advent the interplay of cosmic forces appears wholly unconcerned.

It is indeed very difficult to estimate the extent to which our merely physical existence collaborates with the forces

[1] Wisdom i. 7.   [2] Ibid., viii. 1.

of the universe. It may be of little importance, though our body must play some part in the regulation of the world's energies. But there is another aspect of our creative process which requires indispensably our spiritual activity. We cannot but think that the mysterious impulse which pervades all beings and pushes forward their material evolution by releasing in them such a passion for existence, such a determination to live, proves by its very power and permanence, and by the indomitable violence of its explosion that an infinite value is concerned here and that at the heart of the process a fire is burning.

In any case it seems reasonable to hold that the immense will to exist which works like a leaven throughout nature aspires to a calm when its tumultuous energies mysteriously spiritualised, will find their expression *in quality* in the transparence of a countenance completely open and in the light of a look which concentrates at a single diaphanous point the depths of all the seas.

The universe is no doubt justified when a Saint is born anywhere. Sanctity crowns with freedom the titanic jubilee of the forces which fashion matter. In man, in whom every creature is summed up,[1] the boundless dream which they dimly pursue becomes conscious of its mystery and a passage is opened at last to the Reality, still nameless, whose irresistible attraction they undergo.

Certainly man must consent to efface himself before It. But when he yields and surrenders himself irrevocably to Its grasp, the world itself is set free[2] in a soul dispossessed of herself in whom the vital forces unchained in the Universe

---

[1] *In Ascens.* Dom. 9th L. Hom. S. Gregory.
[2] Again we have in mind St. Francis and his Canticle of the Sun. Cf. Rom. viii. 20–22.

are interiorised, stripped and gathered up in a silent adherence to the sovereign demands of the last End.[1]

What is It in Itself, and in what ways does It act? It is less important to know the answer than to be open to Its invitations. Souls who have given an unreserved consent at any time or in any place have all *adhered*, implicitly at least, to the mystery of the Cross, in which the Love which attracts all to Itself has willed to reveal its depths.

And all now share in the mystery of the altar, where the same sacrifice is perpetuated down the ages, together with those scriptural heroes chosen as types of their fidelity and pledges of our hope : Abel, Abraham, Melchisedech.

Upon these gifts vouchsafe to look with a favourable and serene countenance and to accept them, as Thou wert graciously pleased to accept the gifts of Thy righteous servant Abel, and the sacrifice of our patriarch Abraham, and that which Thy high priest Melchisedech offered to Thee a holy sacrifice, a spotless victim.

These few words bring before us the entire course of Religion, its continuity from first to last, the mysterious unity of history, the spiritual meaning of the universe, the perpetuity of hope and the eternity of Love.

[1] It is in fact under this aspect that the Divine Reality is revealed in the aspiration whose course we are attempting to trace.

SUPPLICES

CREATION is not confined to the visible universe.

The stupendous variety of which the latter affords us the spectacle is but a feeble image of the riches comprised in the world of pure spirits.

Since God is Spirit, it would be inconceivable that He had not first created a spiritual universe in His image before[1] impressing on matter the imprint of His glory, or that this spiritual universe could be confined to that lowest degree, in which spirit is so closely bound up with matter, represented by our humanity. On the contrary it must be incomparably richer, more various and lovelier than the visible world.

Faith confirms these expectations, suggested to reason by its perception of values and demand for harmony. This is the meaning of our belief in *Angels*.

We must not form material images of beings whose nature has nothing of quantity. It will not be difficult, if we are not so naïve as to confine the creation to what the eyes can behold, to understand how immensely our vision of the Universe is enlarged by this mysterious Scriptural doctrine.

Not only do all the energies of cosmic life invade us as they ceaselessly stream in upon us ; we are also constantly subjected to the elevating or seductive suggestions made by the world of pure spirits, good and evil. Our free-

[1] In the order of intention, not necessarily in the order of duration (or time).

will, it is true, possesses an inviolable power to accept or reject the latter, which it does not possess in regard to the cosmic influences to which our organism is exposed. But the fact that it is precisely our free choice which is at stake in the contest whose issue is its determination to good or evil, since God's entire work depends upon our consent, does but render more moving the unseen duel continually being fought out in the arena of our souls.

The Charity ' shed forth in our hearts by the Holy Spirit that has been given to us ' enables us, however, as Its life grows in our hearts, to escape the maleficent suggestions—for the spirit of evil is blind to love—while remaining open to the good influences.

What could be more consoling than to think of the glorious alliances and noble friendships we can contract with the faithful Angels by the silent mediation of prayer.

The prayer on which we are meditating implores their intervention to carry to the heavenly altar the oblation offered upon ours, giving to their multitude a concrete shape in the Angel who appeared to the seer of Patmos standing before the altar, a golden censer in his hand.[1]

Obviously this heavenly altar is a symbol. What is no symbol is the saving activity of the heavenly spirits, their constant vigilance and unfailing charity, and their unseen participation in the Liturgy. This surely is the most fitting moment to renew our friendship with our exalted brothers, the Angels.

We humbly beseech Thee, Almighty God, command these things to be borne by the hands of Thy holy Angel to Thine altar on high, in the sight of Thy Divine Majesty; that as

[1] Apoc viii. 3

many of us, as by participation at this altar shall receive the most Sacred Body and Blood of Thy Son, may be filled with every heavenly blessing and grace. Through the same Christ our Lord. Amen.

Christ's offering, it is true, possesses *in itself* an infinite value to which the Angels' intercession can add nothing. It is only our limited capacity to receive that can restrict its efficacy.

And with good reason we fear that our hearts are too small for so great a gift.

MEMENTO OF THE DEAD

'GOD is not a God of the dead, but of the living.'[1] The dead have disappeared from our sight. They have not disappeared from the sight of God. He knows where they are, He knows their lot, He 'who loved them unto the end.' But, can we meet them, can we communicate with them?

Some of them occupied such a large place in our life; they were the light of our eyes, the source of our happiness, the soul of our soul. Is all this now finished for ever?

How can it be finished, if man is more spirit than flesh, and if we have truly been in communion with what was most intimate and spiritual in them?

But how shall we find them again? By what means shall we reach them? By entering into what is most intimate in ourselves?

If in truth they sleep in Christ, as we may always hope, they are certainly freed from the divisions of space and time, from all material constraints, from all the changes of *the outer world*. There is, therefore, no means of meeting them, more certainly efficacious, than to establish ourselves on that *internal* plane which they have reached, and strive to live their life. Since their life is plunged deep in the interior of God, since He is their home, their food and as our prayer so touchingly expresses it, their sleep, if we identify ourselves more closely with Him, and enter more

[1] Matt. xxii. 32.

deeply into *His Life*, we shall enter into *their life*, and the converse broken off on the visible plane will be resumed in a more living fashion in the silent commerce of souls.

It is indeed *within* that we must seek, if we would not go astray in a world beyond, constructed with shadows of the visible world, imagining relations with our dear ones which would tend to hold them back on the external plane, from which *already on this side of the grave* if our spiritual life is to progress, we must free ourselves ever more perfectly. If they are withdrawn from the vicissitudes of the sensible world, have been born[1] to the Life of the Spirit, are in God, we cannot conceive a bond between ourselves and them more sublime than the communion, always closer, of an inner life of which God is the source, the centre and the gift.

In this way our love not only safeguards its profound reality, it is also most efficacious. For by the strength of our love for God we can in a sense give Him to our departed, if they are still detained in the stages of purification which constitute the mysterious state of Purgatory; or increase in some way their joy in possessing Him, if they have already reached the beatific vision.

To live so as to be always worthy of God, this surely is the most certain way to be always with our dead.

There can be no doubt that for their part they have lost nothing of their affection for us *which deserved to live eternally*. We may therefore be assured that their desire for intimate union with us, be it understood for union in a love perfectly true, is far greater than even our own desire for it. For they are in God, the very heart of Love.

---

[1] Born in the sense of 'natale'—birthday, as used in the martyrology, the day of death.

But we also may approach this Divine Love, for it is in God ' that we live, and move and exist '.[1] We also are in God, though not yet so completely as they. And God is in us. But God is the heaven of faithful souls. Heaven therefore is in us in so far as God is there.

May we not conclude that our soul is a sanctuary of the holy souls as it is a temple of God ?   Are we not justified in thinking that we bear them after a fashion in ourselves and that they are incomparably closer to our soul than the little babe of which she is the tabernacle is close to its mother's heart ? Christ exceeded our most daring hopes by making the circumincession[2] of the Divine Persons the bond of our mutual intimacy ' that they may be one, even as Thou and I are one '.[3]

There can be no surer comfort than this active and sanctifying communion with our dear ones in an intimacy continually increasing as our union with God becomes closer. God has not taken them from us : He has hidden them in His heart that they may be closer to ours.

' God is not a God of the dead but of the living '.

Be mindful also, O Lord, of thy servants and handmaids who are gone before us with the sign of faith and sleep the sleep of peace, *N* and *N*. To them, O Lord, and to all who rest in Christ, grant, we beseech Thee, a place of refreshment, light and peace. Through the same Christ our Lord. Amen.

Let us ask God that our loves may be such now that they can endure everlastingly, and let us enlarge our commemoration of the departed by bringing into it all the dead whose deaths are reported in to-day's paper, all the

[1] Acts xvii. 28.   [2] The mutual inhabitation.   [3] John xvii. 21–22.

souls for whom no one will pray, all the heroes of history[1] whose names are written in our hearts. For they have not ceased to exist and they live beyond the veil which shrouds in darkness man's final destiny, that it may be wholly entrusted to God.

[1] Prayer for the great figures of history would be an excellent way to make children realise 'the continuity of religion', the efficacy of prayer and the Communion of Saints.

NOBIS QUOQUE PECCATORIBUS

In the lowest rank of the assembly which unites all ages, all worlds and all souls the priest at last mentions himself, calling himself with raised voice a sinner, and smiting his breast like the publican.

He knows only too well how unworthy he is of the sacramental identification in virtue of which he permanently *represents* the person of Christ. Therefore he never ceases to prostrate himself in spirit before those words in which Christ says I by his mouth, before the words pregnant with the Divine pardon, before the souls that call him father and credit him with the light which their generosity kindles in him, before all those sufferings he has not assuaged, before all those abandoned souls after whom he has not gone in search, before the entire world which looked to him for its redemption. Above all he is prostrate in the lowest rank of sinners before the great Pauper whose honour he has accepted but whose reproach he has refused to bear.

Nobis Quoque Peccatoribus : to us sinners also. He realises how true this accusation is. For he is confronted with the supreme abdication of his God. How empty all his sermons now appear when the eternal Word has become silent, and how sorry are his claims to respect when the Lord and Master has chosen the lowest place for Himself.

De multitudine miserationum Tuarum sperantibus : expecting everything from the superabundance of thy mercies.

Is not wretchedness the proper object of mercy? 'The more gladly,' said St. Paul, ' will I glory in my weaknesses that the power of Christ may dwell in me.'[1]

A wonderful refuge indeed! How perfectly the cure fits the malady! The light which discovers the wound is also the love that heals it. ' Simon, son of Jonas, lovest Thou Me more than these?'[2] With gentle irony and a kindly smile these words recall, so tactfully, the proud boast, followed by such emphatic denial. 'Though all should be scandalised (in Thee) yet shall not I.'[3] But the Apostle still dares to reply: 'Lord, Thou knowest all things, Thou knowest that I love Thee.'[4] 'When thou wast young, thou didst gird thyself and go whither thou wouldst; when thou art old thou shalt stretch forth thine arms and another shall gird thee and lead thee whither thou wouldst not.'[5]

At bottom the essence of every sin is to will to be of oneself, what one can be only in God, what God alone can be in us, since for us, to live is to let Him live in us, because in truth to *be* is *to give oneself*. The matter is luminously clear. Sin is the return of a being on itself, the appropriation to self which renders it impenetrable to the light, the possession that imprisons it within itself, dooming it to an appalling barrenness, whereas humility is the aperture through which it issues forth and expands, gathering up every illumination it receives.

O God, to be! Might we but be as Thou art, whose Being is eternally outpoured, whose vision is ineffably simple, whose Love is infinitely translucent as Thou art in the Poverty thrice subsistent of Thy Persons.

---

[1] 2 Cor. xii. 9.   [3] Mark xiv. 29.   [5] John xxi. 18.
[2] John xxi. 15.   [4] John xxi. 17.

But we may yet be reborn in such an existence, reborn this very day, by humble confession, reborn in the joy of destitution, the destitution He chose for His cradle.

To us sinners also, Thy servants who trust in the multitude of Thy mercies, vouchsafe to grant some part and fellowship with Thy holy apostles and martyrs ; with John, Stephen, Matthias, Barnabas, Ignatius, Alexander, Marcellinus, Peter, Felicitas, Perpetua, Agatha, Lucy, Agnes, Cecilia, Anastasia, and all Thy Saints ; into whose company we beseech Thee to admit us, not weighing our merit but freely pardoning our offences. Through Christ Our Lord.

THE DOXOLOGY

THE saints' intercession derives all its value from the mediation of Christ. Their prayers are lost in His, as rivers in the sea. His name has concluded all our prayers as identification with His Person has been throughout the sole aim of the Liturgy.

The Canon concludes with a doxology in which Christ in His character as mediator is exalted with a wealth of language which recalls the concentrated rapture of St. Paul's Christology.

All good things *descend* from the Father through Jesus, and all glory *reascends* through Jesus to the Father. That is to say, Jesus is at once God giving Himself to man and man giving himself to God, being thus the confluence of two loves exchanging their utter poverty. God becomes the Guarantor and the Debtor of humanity's debt, a humanity which is here nothing but a response to the appeal of his love. God extends to humanity the mysterious altruism of Self[1] that is pure donation, since *human nature* is now but a holocaust consumed by the Divine fire, a living altruism in its relation to the Godhead that is its true Self. The Canon ends with this encounter in which the mystery of the Cross reveals its depths : God crucified in man and man crucified in God, in the unity of one Person, a Divine Person.

Behold and see if there be any sorrow like unto Mine.[2]

[1] Here the Self is the Personality or subsistence of the Word.   [2] Lam. i. 12.

Christians have never ceased to hear this appeal and ' to look on Him whom they have pierced.'[1]

Though they have not ceased to combat under all its forms the evil which is the origin of suffering, they have accepted the latter ' as a Divine cure of our defilements '. Nothing perhaps could reveal more palpably the presence of Christ and the perpetuity of His action than the words spoken by a labourer afflicted with an incurable disease. His face radiant with an inner light, he said as though it were obvious, ' Surely *we* can suffer since the Good God has suffered.' There could be no sublimer theology.

Nor is Christ a figure of past history. We meet Him every day in the depths of souls.

By whom, O Lord, Thou dost always create, sanctify, quicken, bless and give us all these good things.

These good things[2] are everything we have received in the orders of nature and grace, all that has been made; received in their very Source, under the figure of the consecrated elements designated by a triple sign of the cross. What thanksgiving can befit such a Gift, save the Gift Itself?

By Him and with Him and in Him, all honour and glory are Thine, O God the Father Almighty, in the unity of the Holy Ghost for ever and ever. Amen.

Of old at this point a deacon lifted the two-handled chalice large enough to communicate the faithful under the

---

[1] John xix. 37.   Cf. Zech. xii. 10.
[2] Cf. Duchesne, *Origines*, pp. 193-194. Batiffol, *Leçons sur la Messe*, pp. 272-274. Fortescue, *The Mass*, pp. 471-473.

species of wine[1] while the Pope elevated the consecrated Bread. Their movements coincided and fused in a single *Gesture of Offering* which was the most striking comment upon the Doxology. Of this rite we have kept the conjunction of the two species during which five signs of the cross are made, followed by their simultaneous elevation.[2]

We offer the Father what is dearest to Him and our own most valuable possession, at the same time setting before ourselves the programme of a life which will complete in us the mystery of the altar.

By Him, with Him, in Him.
Amen.

[1] About the ninth century, however, for the communion of the people the consecrated wine was poured in small quantities into cups, scyphi, containing unconsecrated wine diluted with water. Batiffol, op. cit., pp. 94–95, Cf. p. 88.

[2] Incorrectly termed the little elevation. The object of the double elevation of the Host and Chalice is to show the people the consecrated gifts and present them to their worship, whereas we have here a ceremony of offering which presents them to God in accordance with the intention of the Doxology.

NOTE ON THE SAINTS OF THE CANON

(A) IN THE COMMUNICANTES

After our Lady and the Apostles this list mentions St. Peter's first three successors, Linus, Cletus or Anacletus, and Clement. Clement is famous for his epistle to the Corinthians written about 95–6 on the occasion of dissensions which had arisen in their Church. It contains (chapters 59–61) one of the finest examples of liturgical improvisation which have come down to us. Xystus II (the name is also written Sixtus), Pope under the Emperor Valerian (254–260), arrested while presiding at the Liturgy in the cemetery of Pretextatus, was beheaded about August 6th, 258. Cornelius, probably a member of the gens Cornelia and thus a descendant of Sulla, was banished under Gallus to Centumcellae (Civita-Vecchia) where he died in 253. He was in close correspondence with Cyprian of Carthage who wrote to congratulate him on the glory of his 'confession'. 'If either of us, prevented by God's mercy, should precede the other in death may our friendship continue in the Lord and our prayer to the merciful Father for our brethren and sisters never cease' (Eph. lx. 2).

Cyprian, himself an advocate, converted to Christianity about 246, who became bishop about 250, was one of the noblest characters of Christian antiquity. His authority in the Church about the middle of the third century may be compared with that exercised by St. Ambrose towards the end of the fourth. Unfortunately he became involved in an inextricable dispute with Pope Stephen on the question of heretical baptism whose validity he attacked with arguments which built too confidently on the images he employed. 'The Church like the garden of Paradise contains fruit trees enclosed by its walls. . . She waters these trees with the water of four rivers, namely the four gospels, whence she pours forth a saving and heavenly flood, the grace of baptism. How can anyone water from the springs of the Church who is not in the Church ?' (Ep. lxxiii. 10, 13). Pope Stephen, held by the traditional practice of his Church : '*Nihil innovetur nisi quod traditum est.*' Cyprian, however, recognised that 'it was on Peter first that the Lord founded His Church and in whom he established and made manifest the origin of her unity and to whom he gave the power whereby that shall be (truly) loosed on earth which he (Peter) has loosed' (Ep. lxxiii. 7–1). But he thought Peter had yielded at Antioch to Paul's remonstrance (Ep. lxxiii. 1) and believed that it was his duty to play St. Paul's part towards Stephen. The dispute threatened to lead to a schism when Stephen died. Cyprian, banished to Curubis a few days later, was sentenced the following year to be beheaded. 'Are you Thascius Cyprianus ?' the proconsul Galerius Maximus asked him. 'I am,' replied the Bishop. 'Are you the Pope of the impious ?' 'I am.' 'The most sacred Emperors order you to sacrifice.' 'I will not.' 'Think of yourself.' 'Do what is commanded you ; the matter is too clear for consideration.' The Proconsul concluded : " Thascius Cyprianus must be put to death by the sword.' Then the Bishop Cyprian replied, 'Thanks be to God.' The execution was carried out the same day. Cyprian, wearing a linen tunic, awaited the executioner, told his friends to give him twenty-five gold pieces, bandaged his own eyes and received the fatal blow, September 14th, 258.

LAWRENCE, Xystus' deacon, suffered martyrdom a few days later than he, August 9–10, 258.

CHRYSOGONUS, a Greek by birth, lived at Rome in the reign of Diocletian (285–305). He suffered martyrdom at Aquileia.

JOHN AND PAUL, officials of Constantius II, were beheaded in their house on the Celian at Rome under Julian the Apostate. Such at least is the traditional story. Some think that they suffered in an earlier persecution and that their relics were brought to Rome from the East.

COSMAS and DAMIAN suffered martyrdom at Aegae in Cilicia under Diocletian. Obviously the choice of these latter Saints was due to popular devotion, one of the rare instances in which we can trace its influence in the old Roman Liturgy.

(B) IN THE NOBIS QUOQUE PECCATORIBUS

JOHN, named first, is John the Baptist who was 'a voice, a cry,' and whose life and death are summed up in his own words : ' He that hath the bride is the bridegroom. The friend of the bridegroom stands by and listens to him speak and rejoices to hear his voice. This joy is mine in its fullness. He must increase, I must decrease' (John iii. 29–30. Cf. the story of his martyrdom, Mark vi. 17–30).

MATTHIAS is the Apostle chosen to replace Judas (Acts i. 15–26).

STEPHEN is the first martyr, about the year 36. A young man named Saul took part in his stoning (Acts vii. 58). The grace of Christ for which Stephen prayed with his dying voice made him Saint Paul.

BARNABAS was a Levite from Cyprus, converted very early at Jerusalem (Acts iv. 36–7) who introduced the converted Saul to the Apostles (Acts ix. 27). The Apostles sent him to Antioch where Christ's disciples were first called Christians (Acts xi. 22–6). Recognising Saul's genius, he brought him from Tarsus to Antioch (Acts xi. 25) and undertook with him a mission in Cyprus continued by the first mission in the South of Asia Minor (Acts xiii. 14). Later a dispute divided them (Acts xv. 39) and St. Paul's glory cast into the shade the man who had so generously brought him to the fore.

IGNATIUS, Bishop of Antioch, was condemned to the wild beasts under Trajan about 107. He has left seven magnificent letters overflowing with love for Christ. To the Romans who, he feared, might intervene on his behalf he wrote these inimitable words : ' If you keep silence about me, I shall become a word of God, but if you love my flesh too much I shall again be a mere sound (cf. 1 Cor. xiii. 1). Only allow me to be offered as a libation to God while the altar is still prepared. I am God's wheat and am to be ground by the beasts' teeth to become the spotless bread of Christ. Agree with me. I know what is good for me. Now I begin to be a disciple. My birthday is at hand. Suffer me to come to the pure light. When I reach it I shall be a man indeed. Permit me to imitate the passion of my God. If any man bears Him in himself he surely will understand my desire, and sympathise with me, knowing the constraint laid upon me. (Fleshly) love has been crucified in me and there is no longer fire of love for material things ; but only a living water that speaks to me within my soul. Come to the Father ' (Rom. ii–vii.).

ALEXANDER is probably one of the seven martyrs honoured on July 10, and regarded by later legend as seven sons of the martyr St. Felicitas. Fortescue and Dom Vandaleur prefer to identify him with the first Pope Alexander (106–115).

The exorcist PETER and the priest MARCELLINUS were martyred under Diocletian at a place called the black forest, sylva nigra, known henceforward as the white forest, sylva candida.

FELICITAS and PERPETUA were given to the wild beasts in the amphitheatre of Carthage in the reign of Septimus Severus (193–211) at the opening of the third century. Perpetua displayed an indomitable courage : ' When we had all been sentenced to the beasts,' she writes, ' we returned to prison rejoicing.' And she had a little baby which she suckled in prison. Her biographer relates that having been tossed by a savage cow in the arena she bound up her hair with a brooch so as not to ' enter into glory like a mourner.' Felicitas gave birth to a child in prison, and when the pains made her cry out, one of those present asked her : ' If you cannot bear your pain now, what will you do when you face the beasts ? ' ' It is I who suffer now,' she replied, ' but then another will be in me who will suffer for me, because I shall suffer for Him.'

AGATHA of Catania or Palermo in Sicily was martyred under Decius (251). According to her legend she uttered against the unjust judge who had her breasts cut off the magnificent rebuke : ' Cruel tyrant, are you not ashamed to wound in a woman the breast you sucked in your mother ? '

LUCY of Syracuse was burnt and beheaded under Diocletian about 304.

AGNES ' plighted her troth to the heavenly Bridegroom who fed her with milk and honey ' under Valerian (254–260) or Diocletian (285–305). It is said she was only twelve years old. Legend, however, has more to relate of her than history.

CECILIA was probably martyred under Marcus Aurelius at about 177 when Pothinus, Blandina and their companions suffered at Lyons. Some historians place her martyrdom in the reign of Alexander Severus (222–235). This is most unlikely, since that Emperor was very friendly towards the Christians.

ANASTASIA is said to have suffered at Palmaria in Illyria under Diocletian (295–305). Her name, which means resurrection, is associated with the Dawn Mass of Christmas.

4. HE BROKE IT

THE BREAKING OF BREAD

THE LORD'S PRAYER

TAUGHT by Thy saving precepts and following Thy
Divine instruction we presume to say :

OUR FATHER WHO ART IN HEAVEN,
HALLOWED BE THY NAME.
THY KINGDOM COME.
THY WILL BE DONE
ON EARTH AS IT IS IN HEAVEN.
GIVE US THIS DAY OUR DAILY BREAD.[1]
AND FORGIVE US OUR TRESPASSES,
AS WE FORGIVE THEM THAT TRESPASS AGAINST
  US.
AND LEAD US NOT INTO TEMPTATION,
BUT DELIVER US FROM EVIL.[2]
AMEN.

'When the fullness of time was come God sent His
Son, born of a woman, born under the Law to redeem
those that were under the Law, that we might receive the
adoption of sons. And because ye are sons God hath
placed in your hearts the Spirit of His Son that crieth
Abba, that is Father, so that thou art no longer a slave
but a son and an heir through God.'[3]

'Ye have not received a spirit of bondage unto fear,

[1] 'Daily.' The Greek ἐπιούσιον should, we think, be rendered, befitting,
the bread which satisfies our needs, the necessary, the right portion, the 'appointed
portion.'

[2] Or the Evil One. In the Greek Genitive the Masculine and Neuter genders
have the same form : πονηροῦ. Matt. v. 37 and 39 ; xiii. 19 and 38.

[3] Gal. iv. 6–7.

but have received a spirit of adoption whereby we cry Abba, that is Father.'[1]

'You were formerly darkness, but are now light in the Lord. Walk as children of the light.'[2]

This is Saint Paul's commentary. Christ gave His in the parable of the prodigal Son. 'When his father saw him yet a long way off, his heart was moved and he ran to him and threw himself on his neck and embraced him.'[3]

Our Father : we are His sons in truth, and His life is ours. Your children are His children, and in the soul of this tiny baby whom Baptism has identified with the Only Son you may *visit the Eternal Trinity.* Mothers, your house has become a church, and God has placed in your hands a Monstrance and a Book of Hours.

Our Father : so magnificent is this title that souls sufficiently simple to give it its full significance have attached themselves to it with an inexhaustible devotion, finding heaven in it. When Mère de Ponçonas, foundress of the Reformed Bernardines in Dauphiné, was at Ponçonas during her childhood, she made the acquaintance of a poor girl in charge of cattle who at first seemed so ignorant that she thought she knew nothing of God. Full of zeal she took her aside and began to teach her. This wonderful girl begged her with tears to tell what she should do to finish her Pater noster. For she said in her country parlance, " I can't get through it. For almost five years past when I say the word ' Father ', and consider that He who is up there," as she said this she pointed her finger upwards, " that He is my Father, I weep and remain all day in this state while I watch my cows."[4]

---

[1] Rom. viii. 15.   [2] Eph. v. 8.   [3] Luke xv. 20.
[4] Brémond, *Hist. du Sentiment Religieux*, Vol. II.

How inexorable must be the moral demands whose fulfilment has made it possible for ineffable Love to witness the boundless suffering which has tormented mankind since its beginning. On earth we cannot know why it must be so. The Cross, by making God Himself a partaker of our agony, is our surest guarantee that this suffering is a moral necessity and must be the most mysteriously merciful gift of His love.

If suffering is given us, it is because its hour has come. 'If God gave us masters He had specially chosen, what willing obedience we should owe them. Necessity and events are such infallible teachers.'[1]

We are not, however, forbidden to utter the recoil from suffering which we naturally feel and to ask God with Pope Gregory[2] to be preserved from all evil, past, present and future.

We can ask anything. What God will give us will be the most profitable to us, provided, however, we grasp from within whatever befalls us, making His view of it our own.

Deliver us, we beseech Thee, O Lord, from all evils, past, present and future ; and by the intercession of the blessed and glorious Mary, ever a Virgin, Mother of God, together with Thy blessed Apostles Peter and Paul and Andrew and all the saints, mercifully grant peace in our days : that by Thy helpful compassion we may be always free from sin and secure from all disturbance, through the same Jesus Christ Thy Son, Our Lord, who with Thee in the unity of the Holy Ghost liveth and reigneth God, world without end. Amen.

[1] Pascal, *Mystère de Jésus*, Br. 553.
[2] It was probably this Pope who introduced into the Liturgy the prayer Libera nos Quaesumus Domine, at least in its present form, when he placed the Pater, originally said after the fraction, immediately after the Canon. Cf. Dom Wilmart in Bishop, *Genius of the Roman Rite*, pp. 84–87.

H

THE FRACTION

The Kiss of Peace introduced by the Pax Domini, the breaking of the bread, the recitation of the Pater noster and the reception of the Sacrament, such no doubt was the original order until Saint Gregory changed the place of the Lord's Prayer.

When concelebration was still the practice,[1] the unity which these ceremonies express must have been given an extraordinary prominence. 'As there is but one bread, we, though many, are one body, for we all partake of the same bread.' Of this saying of St. Paul's,[2] the ancient ceremonies were a magnificent illustration.

To show that there is but one bread, the Pope placed in the chalice the *Sancta*, a portion of the bread consecrated at the previous Mass, some days before,[3] being careful to take a fragment from the Host of the present celebration to be reserved similarly for the next Liturgy. He also set apart some fragments which a cleric took to the priests of those more distant titles (parishes) which could not assist at the station Mass.[4]

Thanks to the *Fermentum*, as each of these fragments was called, there was ideally but one Mass the same day,

[1] Down to the ninth century in Rome, at least on the chief festivals. Cf. Duchesne, *Origines*.
[2] 1 Cor. x. 7.
[3] Originally the Liturgy was celebrated only on Sunday, and this practice continued at Rome until the beginning of the fifth century. Duchesne, *Origines*, p. 480.
[4] The solemn Liturgy of the Roman Church, over which the Pope presided, was celebrated at the church announced at the Previous Mass as the Station.

as in virtue of the *Sancta* there was but one Liturgy through-out the succession of Sundays. And there is but the one Christ received under the diverse species, as the ceremony of the *Commixtion* insisted. The Pope before his Com-munion broke off a fragment from the bread just consecrated and let it fall into the chalice, saying the prayer we still recite.

May the sacred commixture of the Body and Blood of Our Lord Jesus Christ be to us who receive it the source of ever-lasting life. Amen.

The breaking of the bread was prefaced by the Kiss of Peace, passed through the entire congregation. Single-hearted charity prepared their souls for the Divine visit. Then the bread was broken. The bishops and priests took part in this function, having first received in linen bags the consecrated bread which acolytes brought them from the altar. From his chair the Pope gave the signal for it, the chant of the Agnus Dei uttered its mystery.[1]

Lamb of God, who takest away the sins of the world, have mercy on us.

Then the Pater was recited and communion given to the chant of an antiphon[2] which controlled its administration.

These ceremonies express the passion for unity which possessed the Church termed by Ignatius of Antioch ' the President of Charity '.[3] In them the enthusiasm of love makes us feel the heart of a mother beating beneath the calm serenity of Roman dignity.

[1] At least since the pontificate of Pope Sergius (687–701). Cf. Duchesne, *Origines*, also Batiffol, *Leçons*, pp. 91–93, 282–287.
[2] Antiphon : ' psalm sung by two choirs '. Duchesne, *Origines*.
[3] Epistle to the Romans. Address.

She remembers Emmaus, the blindness which prevented the disciples recognising their Master until their charity to the wayfarer had opened their eyes.

' *Audiendo ergo praecepta Dei illuminati non sunt, faciendo illuminati sunt.*'

' While they listened to God's commandments they were not enlightened, when they performed them they were. And the God they had not recognised in the explanation of Scripture, they recognised in the breaking of bread.'[1] It was their charity which revealed to them His. If the ceremonies have been slightly altered, this order has not changed. The Spirit of Christ is the same, and charity is always the object of the first commandment.

It is with charity surely that we should begin the initiation of faith and solve its enigmas.

And how much more efficacious our confessions would become, and how much safer the direction of souls, if everything were judged by this infallible rule.

' By this shall all men know that ye are my disciples, if you love one another.'[2]

We are perhaps too much inclined to-day to see in communion an act that concerns only ourselves and which we perform to satisfy our private devotion.

The Liturgy, though it does not forget the inviolable privilege of our private converse with God, desires nevertheless to foster in us a concern for all our fellows. It never loses sight of the mystical body whose inexhaustible food is Our Lord's Sacred Flesh. Communion therefore,

[1] Monday in Easter week. Homily of St. Gregory at Matins. 3a l. The order of his sentences has been reversed.
[2] John xiii. 35.

if we are to be faithful to its spirit, must be an act of the mystical body acting in us, even more than the private property of our soul. That is to say, the personal identification with Christ at which we aim will be the more complete the more perfectly we have observed in our heart the catholicity of Christian prayer.

How much easier, more comprehensive and nobler the fulfilment of our Easter duty would be, if the faithful were invited to communicate in the ' person ' of the Church and for the entire communion of Saints!

This surely is the meaning of the magnificent prayer which now follows our breaking of bread and introduces the Kiss of Peace.

Lord Jesus Christ, who didst say to thine Apostles : My peace I give unto you, My peace I leave with you, regard not our sins but the faith of Thy Church, and vouchsafe to grant her the peace and unity agreeable to Thy will who livest and reignest God world without end. Amen.

It would be difficult to imagine a purer prayer or a prayer which would better interpret to our limited understanding Jesus' prayer for unity.[1]

It is the prayer expressed of old in such moving language by a primitive Syrian Liturgy which appeals to the natural symbolism of the sacramental sign.

' As this bread (now) broken, once scattered (in the ears of corn) on the hills, has become one, so may the Church from the extremities of the earth be gathered into Thy Kingdom.'[2] If we are attempting to carry out this teaching in our lives, and do not forget ' that we are members one of another '[3] we can now enter without misgiving into the

[1] John xvii. [2] The Didaché. [3] Eph. iv. 25.

more individual sphere of our personal needs and unworthiness.

Lord Jesus Christ, who by the will of the Father and with the co-operation of the Holy Ghost hast given life to the world by Thy death, deliver me by this most Holy Body and by Thy Blood from all my sins and from all evils, make me to adhere always to Thy commandments and never suffer me to be separated from Thee who with the Father and the Holy Spirit livest and reignest God world without end. Amen.

' Jesus Christ
Jesus Christ

I have left Thee, have fled from Thee, denied Thee, crucified Thee.
May I not be separated from Thee for ever.
But we can keep Jesus with us only by the means taught in the Gospel.
Complete and delightful renunciation.'

Thus Pascal wrote in his Memorial. Even more ardent in its brevity was the cry of the dying Giacopone da Todi : ' Io piango perchè l'amore non è amato ', ' I weep because Love is not loved.'

Let me therefore lose myself in Thee, O Lord, and separate myself from everything which separates me from Thee.

May the Communion of Thy Body, O Lord Jesus Christ which I presume to receive, altogether unworthy though I am, not turn to judgment upon me and condemnation, but become through Thy mercy a safeguard and a remedy for my soul and body, O Thou who livest and reignest with God the Father in the unity of the Holy Ghost, God for ever and ever Amen.

5. AND HE GAVE IT TO HIS DISCIPLES

THE COMMUNION

'My flesh is meat indeed, my Blood is drink indeed.'[1]

This was so unequivocal a declaration that many of His disciples could not accept it. 'This is a hard saying; who can hear it?'[2] Had they perhaps divined what we are so naturally tempted to forget; that the Eucharist is a Sacrifice as well as a Sacrament, even perhaps a Sacrament to the degree in which it is a Sacrifice, the Sacrifice of the Cross in the heart of the Church, that is in our hearts and in our lives *by the adherence of our entire being to the crucified Messiah Who gives us for food His Passion?*

'Whenever you eat this bread and drink this chalice you show forth the Lord's *death* until He come.'[3]

Was not this the meaning just now of that mysterious invasion of our lips by the Divine Self: This is *My* Body? This is *My* Blood?

If these words are to possess their full reality, if they are not to ring false on our tongues, surely the consecration must be after a fashion as it unlooses their matter and thus separates bread and wine from their substance—the symbol of our disappropriation, the *sacrament* of the dispossession, *of the Divesting of our self*, even as now the eating of the sacred Species is *the Sacrament* of our wholly *interior* and

[1] John vi. 55.
[2] John vi. 6. Cf. Friday within the Octave of Corpus Christi, VIIIth lesson. 'Non enim cogitabant haec audiendo, nisi carnem quod ipsi erant,' Sermo S. Augustini: 'When they heard these words they thought only of flesh such as they were themselves.'
[3] 1 Cor. xi. 26.

purely spiritual assimilation to the Saviour who comes to take possession of our soul, *The sacrament of our clothing with Christ.*[1]

To eat the flesh of the Son of Man and to drink His Blood is therefore to live this entire mystery on the mystical Alvernia where our soul is crucified, stripped of self and reclad with Christ. The consecration and the communion are *ideally* inseparable, and the Host always retains an essential relationship to the Cross.

The Kingdom of God is no less sublime now than when Jesus taught in Galilee, and if it is desirable that Communion should become more frequent, indeed daily, this must not be effected at the cost of its essential meaning.

'This is a hard saying, and who can hear it.'

But it is Thy word, O Lord and Thy word is everlasting life. What risk can I run by casting myself into Thy depths ?

I will take the bread of heaven and I will call upon the Name of the Lord.

Though my soul be poor, it is open to Thee, like Zacheus' house, that Thou mayest live Thy life in it, in flooding it with Thy light.

Lord, I am not worthy that Thou shouldest come under my roof, but only speak the word and my soul shall be healed.

With the Host which he holds in his hand the priest makes the Sign of the Cross in front of him, saying :

[1] 'Yield yourself to Jesus Christ,' said Père Condren to the priest, 'not only to sacrifice Him in His intention and in His Spirit, but also in His name and in His person. For we should annihilate ourselves in this action, be in it but pure members of Jesus Christ, offering and performing that which He performs and offers, as if we were not ourselves. We cannot obliterate ourselves too much in this Holy Mystery, nor say sufficiently simply in Jesus Christ : Hoc est Corpus Meum.' (Brémond, *Literary History of Religious Thought*, Vol. III, p. 348.)

' The Body of Our Lord Jesus Christ keep my soul unto life everlasting. Amen.'

Then he uncovers the chalice and gathering up the crumbs of the precious banquet, letting them fall into the chalice, he says :

' What shall I return unto the Lord for all He hath given me ? I will take the cup of salvation and will call upon the name of the Lord. I will call upon Him, and praise Him, and I shall be saved from my enemies.'

He takes the chalice and, making a sign of the cross in the air, he says :

' The Blood of Our Lord Jesus Christ keep my soul unto life everlasting. Amen.'

In their turn the faithful communicate, raising towards the priest eyes like those of the Apostles on Tabor intent upon the Host.

THE COMMUNION ANTIPHON

ON his return to the altar the priest takes the ablutions to guard from all profane touch whatever his hands or lips may have retained of the Sacred Species. He cleanses his lips.

What we have received with the mouth may we receive in spirit[1] that the temporal gift may become our eternal remedy.

He cleanses his fingers.

May Thy Body, O Lord, and Thy Blood which I have received, cleave to every fibre of my heart, and may sin leave no further trace in my soul which Thy holy mysteries have renewed, O God that livest and reignest for ever and ever. Amen.

These acts have a symbolic meaning. Nothing is *in itself* profane or impure. The Divine Presence is the source of all being and in it ' everything is life '. It is the use we make of them that renders things morally good or evil. Nevertheless, particular associations of images or ideas have embodied our moral attitude, and objects have become a language. It is therefore normally by employing symbols rightly that we produce or express the right relationship between our interior life and the world about us.

[1] Cf. Battifol, *Leçons*, p. 17.

Our care for the least fragments of the Lord's Supper shows the value we attach to it, and fosters that scrupulous love whose shrine is reverence.

The same sentiment dictates our reverence for the instruments of the liturgy, as though they still retain the living imprint of the mystery accomplished.

It is for this reason that the priest now reverently spreads the veil over the chalice, as Veronica's handkerchief over Christ's lacerated Face, while the choir sing the communion *antiphon*. Once this was a psalm, sung presumably in the same fashion as the Introit and continued till all the people had communicated.

To-day it has been reduced to an antiphon, or when that has disappeared to one or two verses, taken most commonly from the Psalter. Even so its words and melody alike preserve an inexpressible beauty.

The sparrow hath found her a dwelling
and the turtle-dove a nest in which to lay her young;
(And I) Thine altars, O God of Hosts, my King and my God.
Happy are they that dwell in Thy house;
for ever and ever they shall praise Thee.[1]

This is the moment when the soul rests in God as John rested at the Supper on his Master's heart.

In His shadow for whom I longed,
I have sat down,
And His fruit is sweet to my taste.[2]

Thus the soul experiences the intoxicated ecstasy of the Canticle in the translucent ardour of a love Divinely calm,

[1] Third Sunday in Lent.　　[2] The Heart of Mary.

which invests with a sacramental transparence the passionate appeals of the Biblical Marriage Song. She experiences it in the mysterious solitude of the most personal intimacy, yet in an act of universal communion.

We are always alone even in Church, though at the same time inseparable from others, since we are in touch with them in God who, it is true, makes all souls present to each other because they are touched by the same life-giving breath of His Spirit, but by opening to each one the infinite space of His Heart. They touch but in a liquid atmosphere where each draws breath with a marvellous freedom, enveloped by a limitless love as individually given to each as it is common to all.

Art and science indeed become the wealth of all to the degree in which they express a more intimate personal experience. Mystical union must surely be a far more inviolable secret—a secret of the most inaccessible intimacy, whose intimacy increases as the action of its rays penetrates more deeply the world of souls. Hence this mysterious envelopment by Christ the Host, in which silence becomes so intense that it seems the very beating of His Heart in our own, is necessarily the source of the most fervent intercessions and an all embracing concern.

> Taste and see how the Lord is sweet;
> Happy is the man who
> putteth his trust in Him.[1]

But it is not enough to invite all souls; the entire universe must witness to His Presence, the whole of nature rejoice at His coming.

[1] Eighth Sunday after Pentecost.

Bud forth, flowers, like the lily,
and yield your scent,
offer the beauty of your foliage,
and the praise of your song,
and bless the Lord in His works.[1]

It will not be always thus. We shall not be able to live continually at this jubilant pitch of Corpus Christi. Dryness will come, and the bitterness of desolation, when we shall be obliged once more to arouse the Saviour from His sleep, to behold the danger of His own.

Hear my cry, give ear to my prayer, my King and my God. For it is to Thee that I make my supplication, O Lord.[2]

Remove from me insult and scorn,
For I have sought Thy law, O Lord,
and Thy words have nourished my meditation.[3]

Incline Thine ear (to me).
Make haste to deliver me.[4]

But how can the chalice be taken from us, when the Only Son was not spared it?

Father, if this cup may not pass but I must drink it, Thy will be done.[5]

'Subject to a torment inflicted upon Him by a Hand not human but almighty, Jesus is alone on earth. Not only is there no one to share His suffering, there is none to know it. He endures this agony and dereliction in the horror of night.'[6]

[1] The Rosary.
[2] Second Sunday in Lent.
[3] Ember Friday in September.
[4] Seventh Sunday after Pentecost.
[5] Palm Sunday.
[6] Pascal, *Mystère de Jésus*, Br. 553.

> My heart awaited shame and anguish,
> And I sought for someone to share my sorrow;
> There was none;
> For someone to comfort Me,
> And I found no man.[1]

Love must be prepared to give all and receive nothing. It is in this death of the heart that it attains its perfect truth, and beyond this death that it rises again with eternal depths, as it is by this death that it fully realises its creative fertility, its power of redemption. It will discover, one day, no doubt to its amazement, that at the height of its suffering it has helped Christ who is ' in agony until the end of the world '.[2]

> I was sick and you visited Me;
> in truth I say to you:
> Whenever you did it
> to the least of my brethren
> you did it to Me.[3]

Is not this, perhaps, for certain souls at least, one of the most fruitful lessons of the mystic ' nights ', in which the soul endures that fearful Absence, when God's Presence seems lost for ever and every prayer falls back remorselessly on itself, until at last Faith perceives in the wounded heart of a brother, to whom the entire being bows, the Face which had vanished for a time but was secretly awaiting the soul in the sanctuary of a suffering brother?[4]

When thou canst no longer find Me in your prayer, look for Me in your brethren.

---

[1] Former Mass of the Sacred Heart, ' Miserebitur '.
[2] Pascal, ibid.
[3] S. Camillus de Lellis, July 18.
[4] In this way our neighbour can become for us, on occasion, what may be termed a sacrament of contemplation. Cf. St. Theresa, *The Interior Castle*, Fifth Dwelling, III, 12, and Sixth Dwelling, I. 24.

Tanto tempore vobiscum sum
Et non cognovistis me ?[1]

' So long a time I have been with you and you have
not known me ? '

[1] SS. Philip and James, May 1.

6. THE THANKSGIVING

THE POSTCOMMUNION

CLOSE as He is, God is always ineffable. His gift to us is incomprehensible. His Love is an infinite mystery. No soul will ever exhaust it.

Each one can discover in it that aspect alone which fills his soul. This meeting is therefore unique for every soul and remains her secret.

She must surrender herself in silence and so live. Now or never it is the time to *listen* to the only Word and adhere to It without adding anything of her own, to be a pure assent, a living Amen.

The Liturgy does not presume to dictate to us the sentiments we should have at this moment, or anticipate the wholly unpredictable and perfectly spontaneous discovery which grace may produce in us. On the contrary it wishes to make us completely pliant to the Divine Action by gathering up our entire being in a prayer sufficiently universal to express the thought of all, sufficiently reserved to respect the sovereign liberty of the Holy Spirit. ' For the Spirit helpeth our infirmity. For we know not what we should ask in our prayers, but the Spirit Himself maketh intercession for us with unspeakable groanings.'[1]

Dominus vobiscum, says the priest, thinking that his wish has now been fulfilled with a mysterious completeness. The Lord's Presence is gathering the entire Church into an interior unity almost sensible in this spiritualised atmos-

[1] Rom. viii. 26.

233

phere. How delightful this greeting is now, what joy and what love it expresses!

> The Lord *is* with you.
> *Oremus :* Let us pray.

Filled with Thy sacred gifts, grant, we beseech Thee, O Lord, that we may always continue in thanksgiving.[1]

These few words to celebrate the unutterable Visit! Such are the transports to which Roman piety abandons itself ' in the sober intoxication of the Spirit '. Roman prayer is as bare as the old basilicas whose beauty, devoid of apparent mystery, is exposed wholly legible to the glance, to be penetrated more deeply by every new look, and never to be exhausted. It possesses the same freely chosen poverty as the Gospel accounts of the Passion where no human emotion presumes to mingle with the recital of the Divine tragedy.

Why multiply words when no words can suffice ? The true thanksgiving is a life in conformity with the Mystery just celebrated.

Fed with the delicacies of heaven, we beseech Thee, O Lord, that we may always seek that whereby we truly live.[2]

Life is an internal and autonomous activity, whose origin and end are within itself. How then can we live more intensely and more freely than by constantly identifying ourselves with the Divine Source ?

Guests at Thy holy Table, we have drawn with joy from the fountains of The Saviour ; may His Blood become for us, we beseech Thee, the source of that water that springeth up unto life eternal.[3]

[1] Sunday within the Octave of the Ascension.
[2] Sixth Sunday after the Epiphany.
[3] The Precious Blood.

But this Source opened on the Cross can be poured forth in us only if the Cross itself is planted in our hearts :

We have received, O Lord, the Divine Sacrament, the abiding memorial of Thine immense Love ; grant us, we beseech Thee, to draw from Thy wells, by the merits of St. Paul, and in imitation of him, the water that springeth up unto life everlasting, and in our life and conduct to realise Thy Most Holy Passion imprinted in our hearts.[1]

To be sure God does not take pleasure in the suffering of His children. But He cannot refuse them this share in the mystic birth pangs of His life whereby they are more closely identified with His only Son. Like woman, the soul bears in pain. And her throes are endured not for their own sake but because they open a passage for the new life. The Cross is the tree of life whose mystery is tenderly expressed by the allegory of the vine. 'Every branch that beareth fruit in Me, my Father purgeth that it may bear more fruit.'[2]

We have not to *be* less but on the contrary by an ever more perfect integrity of body and soul to make our being complete.

Grant us, we beseech Thee, O Lord, to find in the reception of Thy holy sacrament refuge for soul and body that, saved in both, we may exult in the fullness of the Divine remedy.[3]

This full and complete being obviously cannot be achieved straight away in a life subject to becoming. It is achieved only by an effort, constantly renewed, to correspond with one's entire being to the gift of each

[1] St. Paul of the Cross, April 28.
[2] John xv. 2.
[3] Eleventh Sunday after Pentecost.

moment by detecting the Divine Reality beneath the veil
of objects.

May Thy Sacraments, we beseech Thee, O Lord, effect in
us what they contain, that we may truly reach the Reality of
that which we enact in figure.[1]

To reach, however, is not to comprehend. Our understanding will be eternally exceeded, and our heart always
be able to rejoice that God is infinitely greater than our
capacity of containing Him. We shall adhere to God
for the sake of God, infinitely beyond our happiness[2] and
to self only as His reflection.

And it is precisely for God, that it is so important that
our soul should preserve the complete transparence of a
window of clear glass and all the spaciousness of a great
cathedral.

O God, who of living and choice stones dost build a dwelling
for Thy Divine Majesty, aid Thy suppliant people, that the
material enlargement of Thy Church may be continued by
her spiritual growth.[3]

Here indeed are the inviolable spaces from which no
captivity can ever debar us, in which our soul breathes
freely the fresh air on the shore of the Divine Ocean. Our

[1] Ember Saturday in September.

[2] Père de Condren has expressed it admirably : ' We are more indebted to God
for that He is His own felicity and goodness than that He renders us blissful
in Him.' (Brémond, *Literary History of Religious Thought in France,* E.T.,
Vol. III, p. 342.) The soul ' should desire to have no part in His (God's)
gifts, which must be only for Him and for His glory and should take her out of
herself and ravish her from herself, rather than bestow something on her, in
order to make her wholly God's . . . so that He alone may live in us in His
own gifts ' (ibid., p. 353). ' It is better to be hidden in God ' (p. 354), to
adhere through Jesus Christ to ' all the UNKNOWN of God ' (p. 341).

[3] The Dedication of a Church.

capacity for love is the measure of our freedom, and though the entire world should attempt to imprison us, it could not prevent our opening our hearts. ' Though the vessels of flesh are constricted, let the spaces of charity be enlarged.'[1]

Joan of Arc on her pyre could still gather the entire Church into her heart, not excluding even her judges from the fire-baptism of her martyrdom.

Pour forth in us, O Lord, the Spirit of Thy love, and in Thy goodness give one single heart to those whom Thou hast fed with the same heavenly bread, through Jesus Christ, Thy Son, Our Lord, who liveth and reigneth with Thee in the unity of the Holy Ghost for ever and ever. Amen.[2]

[1] ' Sed si angustiantur vasa carnis, dilatentur spatia caritatis.' (Office for St. Matthias, 7th Lesson, Sermo S. Augustini.)
[2] For preserving Concord in the Congregation. Among the prayers for Diverse Occasions. 9, Postcommunion.

7. THE PRAYERS OF DISMISSAL

ORATIO SUPER POPULU

A WELL-ORDERED assembly, such as the Christian synaxis,[1] cannot disperse at random. From beginning to end it presupposes the sacrifice of our individual preferences, even the most legitimate. We are present for the sake of our brethren, even more than our own, that we may form together with them one single person in Jesus, praying a single prayer which is Jesus' prayer in the Church. It is therefore unthinkable that we should go away without good reason before the signal to depart has been given. At present the signal is the celebrant's departure from the altar. Different forms of dismissal, however, have succeeded each other in the development of the liturgy, and the Mass retains visible traces of them.

The prayer over the people, ' oratio super populum ', which follows the postcommunion on week-days in Lent, is perhaps a prayer of dismissal. In any case it immediately precedes the dismissal and was originally, it would seem, the only formula of blessing employed in the Roman liturgy.[2]

Possibly the introduction of a blessing after the Ite Missa est has contributed to its disuse. If it has survived on the Lenten ferias (week-days), the reason may be that

---

[1] Synaxis, the Greek equivalent of collecta, assembly, meeting.

[2] That is to say the blessing which at present follows the Ite Missa est is a relatively late addition. Cf. Dom Vandeur, *La Sainte Messe*, p. 296. See, however, the Ordo of St. Amand in Duchesne *Origines*, p. 483. Cf. Batiffol, op. cit., pp. 300–1 ; also Fortescue, pp. 514–515.

the austere liturgy of these days was usually celebrated by a priest to whom a deprecatory formula was better adapted, since blessing in the strict sense was then regarded as an episcopal privilege.

Oremus, prays the priest.

Humiliate capita vestra deo : Bow your heads to God, the Deacon continues.[1]

O God, the Redeemer and friend of innocence, guide unto Thyself the hearts of Thy servants, that conceiving the ardour of Thy Spirit, they may prove firm in faith and fruitful in deed.[2]

This is the authentic style of our collects, and their teaching also, so concise, yet so rich.

O God, who rather than be angry with them that trust in Thee dost prefer to show them mercy,[3] grant us fitly to bewail the evil we have done that we may deserve to obtain the grace of Thy consolation.[4]

Surely it would be impossible to express with greater felicity the boundless hopes which this mercy arouses in us than as they are expressed by this prayer for Tuesday in Holy Week.

May Thy mercy, O Lord, preserve us from every contagion of the old man, and make us capable of a holy newness.[5]

[1] The same formula is found in the *Liturgy of St. John Chrysostom*, ed. de Meester, p. 164. But this blessing is placed before the Communion, as was also the usage of the old Gallican liturgy. Cf. Duchesne, *Origines*, p. 235.

[2] Wednesday after the second Sunday in Lent.

[3] Cf. The Collect for the Tenth Sunday after Pentecost: 'O God, who dost display Thy power principally by forgiving and showing pity, multiply upon us Thy mercy that, hastening towards Thy promises, Thou wouldest make us partake Thy heavenly gifts.'

[4] Saturday after the Fourth Sunday in Lent.

[5] Tuesday in Holy Week.

The Infinite is never exhausted. How could the Divine Countenance become an unchanging image in our hearts? It is always new, always younger, always more beautiful. And every day brings new wonder when we recognise that Face, yet feel that we have never seen It before. It is a new discovery and we experience the joy of a birth.

Therefore the eyes of the soul keep the exquisite limpidity of a child's, and her countenance is fresh because the stamp of time has been effaced by Divine youth of eternity.

Our youth is *in front* of us, we are approaching our birth.

ITE MISSA EST

Missa is the despatch;[1] the despatch of the living poem to the Father whom it celebrates; the despatch of the Children into the Divine harvest of their ' elder Brother '.

' All things are yours, and ye are Christ's, and Christ is God's.'[2] The stars still undiscovered, the nebulae inaccessible to the astronomer, the unknown suns and all the burning travellers along the roads of the sky, the invisible constellations contained in the microscopic sphere of an atom, the mysterious radiations which escape from its wounds[3] and the innumerable waves that link all bodies in the infinite rhythm of that inaudible music which is the unity of the cosmos : all these spaces, all these forces, all

[1] Missa is a form of missio ; despatch or dismissal, here the dismissal of the congregation. Originally there was a double missa, two dismissals, the missa of the catechumens before the Offertory, or, if you prefer, after the Gospel (cf. *Liturgy of St. John Chrysostom*, op. cit., pp. 94–97), and a missa of the faithful after the Communion. For the catechumens were permitted to be present only until the missa catechumenorum ; the baptised on the other hand, unless excommunicated for some sin, must remain until the missa fidelium.

It was therefore quite natural to call the first part of the Liturgy the Missa catechumenorum, the second the Missa fidelium. When the catechumenate ceased to exist, this distinction disappeared with it, and the entire liturgy was called the Missa. This, however, is a purely Western nomenclature. The East has kept the name Liturgy which means a public service, and in particular the service of public worship. Cf. Fortescue, *The Mass*, who explains this point very clearly, reminding us that in St. Benedict's rule Missa was not yet used exclusively of the Mass but means the dismissal concluding any office. Cf. Reg. Cap., XVII, 9, 13, 20, 25, ed. Butler, pp. 47, 48, also Peregrinatio Etheriae in Duchesne's *Origines*, pp. 513 and 516.

The mystical interpretation we have proposed is founded on the inner life of the term, not on its semantic development.

[2] 1 Cor. iii. 23.

[3] Radio-activity results from a spontaneous dissolution of the atom of radio-active elements.

these lifeless beings call upon you; they would fain be a voice in your hymn of praise, a cry of love in your heart; and together with them the animals that roar and bellow in the wilds, the silent creatures of the sea and all the obscure sufferings of the domestic animals.

But our eyes reveal a domain even wider than the kingdom of the fishes and the higher animals, the insects buzzing and humming on their tortuous and untraceable paths through the air, the ants clever, industrious and secretive, the frail butterflies, splendid notes composing a silent music, the birds, those flowers of the air who fill the dawn with their song, and the flowers without wings or voice offering to the light the brilliant chalice of their petals; the entire symphony of these perfumes, colours and sounds, seeks a refuge in your soul.

How much more then the souls of your brethren?

In the first place there are the heroes of history, both those who have left a name and those who are buried in a nameless glory, all the saints, all the mighty, all the weak, all the victims, all the sinners. For in books they belong *to the past*, but in charity they are our *contemporaries*. All these souls are in fact living, and your prayer can still reach them, whether their bones repose in palaeolithic caves or lie in the mud of yesterday's battlefields. From the opposite direction there rises the appeal of those who will come after us, of souls who as yet do not exist and will be the Divine secret of future loves. But above all listen to the appeal of the souls that surround you and whom God will place in your path to-day; those who act through a body and for whom it is your duty to insure food, light rest and health; in short, the joy of living. For bodily hunger makes it impossible to feel the hunger of the soul,

I

and thus suffers Him to famish, who craves to give Himself under the lowly form of bread.

This then shall be your Mass, this shall be your Liturgy, now that you go down from Calvary bearing in your hearts the Ineffable Guest as a Divine leaven; to clothe every creature with His Presence, to incorporate them all into His Being, to make each to the extent of its capacity His Body and His Blood.

Say, I implore you, this *Amen*, which adheres in every creature to all it has of God, be the affirmation which discovers and brings out the best in it, the living smile that opens the gates of light, the mother's face welcoming the First Love.

Go, but the Mass is not finished while a single body hungers, a single soul is tormented, a single heart wounded, a single countenance closed, so long as God is not all in all.[1]

Behold the entire universe is in your hands like a host, to be consecrated by your charity, and restored to its Divine vocation, which is to love and to sing.

' All things are yours, and you are Christ's, and Christ is God's.'[2]

Go, it is the Divine Mission, into God's harvest, to gather all the ears of corn scattered over the hills into one living loaf.

Ite Missa est
Deo Gratias.

[1] 1 Cor. xv. 28.   [2] 1 Cor. iii. 23.

THE BLESSING

FOR the last time the priest bends over the altar.

Accept, O holy Trinity, the homage of my service, and grant that the sacrifice I have offered to Thy Majesty, unworthy though I be, may find favour in Thy sight, and become for me, and all for whom I have offered it, the source of pardon through Christ Our Lord. Amen.

He kisses the holy stone as though to take leave of the *glorious* sepulchre and, turning to the people, says :

'May God Almighty bless you, the Father, the Son and the Holy Ghost. Amen.'

He makes the sign of the cross in the air, thus opening to the entire world the arms of the Cross, which alone are wide enough to clasp it. Infinite in height as in breadth, the Cross emits to the four quarters of heaven the boundless rays of Love.

Who can escape this mysterious embrace? Who will not find refuge in this infinite pardon? This gesture of blessing accompanies all men as a mother's open arms support the child's timid steps. The uplifted hand imparts to every creature the invisible consecration of the Seven Gifts. And the priest feels his heart boundlessly open, mysteriously enlarged, as it were a living cradle of souls.

8. VERBUM CARO FACTUM EST

THE LAST GOSPEL

'You know,' St. Paul wrote to the Corinthians, 'the loving kindness of Our Lord Jesus Christ who, though rich, for our sakes became poor, that by His poverty we might be made rich.'[1]

There could be no finer commentary on this text than the canticle of the Word in St. John's heart:

In the beginning was the Word,[2]
And the Word was with God,
And the Word was God.
He was in the beginning with God.
All things were made through Him,
And without Him was made nothing that hath been made.[3]
In Him was life;
And the life was the light of men.
And the light shineth in the darkness,
And the darkness hath not overcome it.
There was a man sent from God,
Whose name was John.
He came for witness,
To witness concerning the light,
That all might believe through him.
He was not the light,
But was to witness concerning the light.

---

[1] 2 Cor. viii. 9.
[2] The eternal Word, the Only Son, who is in the bosom of the Father.
[3] Adopting a different punctuation, we may also translate, 'And without Him was made nothing. Whatever hath been made was life in Him and the life was the light of men.'

It was the true light[1]
Which enlighteneth every man
That cometh into the world.[2]
He was in the world,
And the world was made through *Him*,
And the world knew Him not.[3]
He came to what was His,
And His own received Him not.
But to as many as received Him
He gave power to become children of God ;
To them that believed in His name,
That were begotten not of blood, nor of the will of the flesh,
Nor of the will of man,
But of God.[4]
And the Word was made flesh,
And dwelt amongst us,
And we beheld His glory,
Glory as of the only-begotten from the Father,
Full of grace and truth.

He *was* in the world, and nevertheless He *came* into the world. He filled everything because everything was life in Him. But His very glory veiled Him from eyes plunged in their darkness, and the splendour of the gift concealed the Giver's hand.

But He was love, and love is revealed only to love, as it is by love alone that He can reign. We thought Him absent when He stood at the door of our hearts, love's

[1] Literally it *was* the light, the true light that enlighteneth every man *coming* into the world.

[2] Two translations are possible. That given above by the Westminster Version, agreeing with the Vulgate and with the Authorised Version. The other is ' it was the true light that coming into the world enlighteneth every man '. This is the rendering preferred by the author. I have, however, followed the Westminster version of this passage.—*Author's note adapted by the translator.*

[3] In his verse the term, phos, light, suddenly yields place to Logos, Word, a change expressed by the passage from the neuter to the masculine.

[4] Begotten of God. Everyone should try to hear in his own soul the infinite mystery of these words.

silent offering. Then He issued from His silence to be in time the living Word that publishes in letters of Blood the infinitely free gift of eternal Charity. He issued from His silence, that is to say, without ceasing to be the Invisible and the Ineffable. But He expressed its mystery by what is most obscure and most silent here below, poverty, holiness and death.

> He came to what was His,
> And His own received Him not.

The mystery of our free will could not find more tragic expression than this text, the power which is ours to banish ourselves from God Himself. He will respect that freedom. Henceforth even poorer and more silent beneath the form of the Host He will continue through the centuries begging, the beggar of love.

'Behold I stand at the door and knock. If any man will hear My voice, and open the door to me, I will come in, and I will sup with Him and He with me.'[1]

[1] Apoc. iii. 20.

III

FONS AQUAE SALIENTIS
IN VITAM AETERNAM[1]

A fountain of water springing up unto everlasting life.[1]

[1] John iv. 14.

1. AT THE CRADLE OF SYMBOLISM

CARO VERBUM FACTA EST[1]

THOSE who look from outside through the windows of a cathedral see nothing of the festival of light and colour within. In the same way Catholic dogma will always be an enigma to those who look at it from outside.

Nevertheless every formula of our creed solves a problem of human life.

The facts to be reconciled have not, it is true, always been explicitly distinguished. But as men have given them their utmost value they have always been without any violence reconciled in a comprehensive whole. Instinctively the mysterious order has been attained in which the reconciled opposites pay their tribute to Wisdom and Love. Catholics knew that God did not create the world to abandon it to chaos. And they have taken peaceable possession of things visible and invisible as of a family inheritance.

This was the great victory of faith of which St. John speaks[2] and the hundredfold recompense for all that must be surrendered.

We must examine this claim more closely, to prove that we are not deluding our hunger.

It is widely thought that believers receive heaven for their portion, clever worldlings the earth. This is false, *The earth is part of the Kingdom of God*. That kingdom is an indivisible whole, a synthesis perfect and entire.

[1] The flesh became word.   [2] 1 John v. 4.

259

If a man will not recognise his limits, and refuses to lose himself in a *better* than himself, the earth in turn refuses itself to him and must withhold from him its joys.

This statement may seem exaggerated. At least it proves, you must allow, that we are aware of the problem and of the anguish involved by the effort to unite harmoniously the sensible and the spiritual, to reconcile flesh and spirit.

It is indeed a difficult problem that confronts the conscience when it awakes, and a heavy demand which is made upon it.

For it is impossible to remain neutral. We cannot pretend to shut our eyes to the world of sense. Neither can we ignore the scope of the human will.

To posit a human act is in fact to demand the Infinite. For the object willed is valuable in as much as it is itself the Absolute, or at least inasmuch as it reflects the Absolute. Without this attraction of Absolute value there can be no desire, no action. It follows from this that we can justify our choices only as stages in the attainment of the sovereign Good : which every man pictures as best he can, and everyone terms Happiness.[1]

Woe, therefore, to the objects and persons that we love. We shall leave them no rest until they have disclosed the secret of the depths, until we have drunk from the Spring whence everything proceeds and to which everything returns.

If we would know to what these demands can lead, we have only to turn to Faust. The entire significance of Goethe's tragedy, what we may call its special mission

---

[1] Happiness, however, as here understood, includes that sublime happiness which consists in sacrificing one's happiness, on the supposition that the sacrifice is necessary for the happiness of what is more valuable than oneself.

among the masterpieces of the world's literature, is in fact to lay bare this great mystery and man's impotence to solve it.[1]

The entire visible universe lies in the wine press, and trodden by a giant's feet yields nothing but tears and blood. Objects despoiled, nature violated, are divested of their light and remain opaque.

The Infinite cannot be seen by eyes of flesh, nor grasped by the hands. Another organ of sight is indispensable, another touch. To find the world we must transcend it.

For Deity, though present in creatures, is not their substance but simply their Cause and their eternal Idea, the mysterious light also which they emit, so long as they continue in existence, according to the degree of their transparence.

They themselves indeed cry out to us : climb higher, we are not He, *ipse fecit nos :* He made us.

How should the flower lay claim to her beauty which dies before herself, since she cannot lay claim to her existence, itself fleeting ?

It is but an instant, the vestige of another splendour.

At the first moment you admired, you were perhaps aware that if your delight was so full, it was because in that beauty you were confronted with *Beauty*.

Boundaries were obliterated, transparent matter was no more than a veil of light over the indescribable Countenance.

In a momentary flash you saw the true countenance of things, knew the joy of the universe, met the Infinite.

Signatum est super nos lumem vultus tui, Domine : dedisti laetitiam in corde meo.[2]

---

[1] Cf. Edmond Joly, *Théotokos*, pp. 184–190, and his *Cantique du Vitrol* pp. 159–210.
[2] Ps. iv. 7.

'The light of Thy countenance has risen upon us, O Lord, Thou hast set joy in our hearts.'

It is indeed thus : creatures are endowed with perfections to whose nature we can conceive no limit.[1]

The very notion of them takes us beyond their present realisation towards the boundless Ocean of Being, and what is most perfect in the created order, includes in its own value its value as a symbol. In fact since every being possesses its peculiar excellence, it is essentially a revelation of God.[2]

It is in this way that the Infinite is in creatures. It is thus that everything becomes worthy of veneration, and the world puts on grandeur.

A new earth and new heavens.[3]

But above all there is a new vision, pregnant with love and reverence. Nature no longer defends herself against us, says no longer : *Noli me tangere nondum enim ascendi ad Patrem meum.*[4] Touch me not, for I have not yet ascended to my father.

With man's heart she has ascended to the Father.[5] And man no longer even thinks of plucking the flower, which must wither in his hand.

[1] The 'fourth way' to God, analogy is thus the metaphysical foundation of symbolism.

[2] Cf. Rom. i. 20. A transcendental relationship to God is comprised in the very essence of every creature which leaves it in some way open to God like a mysterious stained window. Symbolism is at the heart of created being.

[3] Apoc. xxi. 17.

[4] John xx. 17.

[5] Obviously such a pure vision, and such freedom in our relations with creatures, presupposes a genuine rebirth, namely that of which we read in the third chapter of St. John (vv. 3–6). The natural symbolism of things can be fully realised only by the supernatural and intrinsically efficacious symbolism of the Sacraments. Nevertheless, natural symbolism leads up to the latter after its fashion and finds in the latter both its fulfilment and its justification.

He knows that he possesses *in spirit* and in truth whatever his eyes behold.

To him each thing is everything.

But He is not the slave of any. For if under the scorching heat of midday the flower withers, the burning rock will in turn reflect for him the face of God.

With even more reason will he take delight in man.

He will tremble with joy when he has relieved the beggar who, he knows, was Jesus Christ.

So he will go on his way through the world singing the canticle of the sun, and actually bringing salvation to men and things : *Dominus vobiscum*, the Lord be with you.

At this point the name of St. Francis obviously occurs to us.

This symbolic vision[1] of the world is not, however, peculiar to him. The humblest old woman who takes holy water, as she enters the church, shares it.

The Church is its source. For the Church tells us that by the power of Christ matter leads us to the Spirit and imparts Him to us.[2]

She invites every creature to praise her Lord,[3] and does not neglect to evoke by her blessings[4] the spiritual resources latent in every creature. Those who see her from outside, unable to credit her with such youth and faith, accuse her of materialising Spirit. In reality *she spiritualises matter* by stamping it with the seal of God.

At this point our relations with the objects of sense lose all danger. We have no longer to divide ourselves with the world around us. And the *unity* effected in our

[1] More correctly this sacramental vision.
[2] The Sacraments.
[3] In the Office.
[4] The Sacramentals.

minds and hearts makes us understand the full reality of that title of *Saviour* which we so justly give

To the Word made flesh
' That flesh might become Word.'[1]

---

[1] Need we say by participation? Cf. St. Augustine's phrase: Factus est Deus homo ut homo fieret Deus. On the vigil of the Epiphany, 4th Lesson. God became man, that man might become God.

MYSTERIUM FIDEI

The Mystery of the Faith.[1]

[1] Words introduced by the Church into the formula by which the wine is consecrated.

THE PLEROMA OF THE CROSS

NOTHING is simpler, more spiritual and more silent than the Mass. No action is so pregnant with Mystery[1] and life.

Those for whom it is but a spectacle will no doubt find the ceremonies strange, the vestments queer and the language unintelligible. And it is indeed true that we are sometimes tempted to regret that all these texts so felicitously chosen from the finest passages of Scripture are not immediately accessible to even the most ignorant of the faithful, the very people who would often understand them best.

In this respect the gorgeous Byzantine liturgies give us a fine example of adaptability by presenting in each national tongue the same unchangeable rite. The Anglican liturgy affords another example. Would the Latin liturgy admit without detriment a similar translation? An affirmative answer would be hazardous. We shall leave open a question we cannot solve, content with reminding our readers that the use everywhere of the same language is a striking symbol of the Church's universal mission.

The bond of unity forged simply by the employment

[1] The term is here used in the sense in which we speak of the Mystery of the Holy Trinity. It is on this sublime plane that the Liturgy places us. The Mass is in the strictest sense a Mystery of faith. For it is inaccessible save to a vision which has been introduced after a fashion into the *vision* which ' searcheth the deep things of God '. And the aim of the entire Liturgy, as it divests us of self and reclothes us with Christ, is to make us share the operations of this Triune Life in which the inexhaustible riches of Being are the eternal gift of Love in the holiest and most unutterable Poverty.

of one liturgical tongue, the species of world-wide father-land it provides so consolingly for priests and laity travelling abroad, amply compensate for the drawbacks of a dead language. Moreover, the complete translations now so widely brought within everybody's reach make it much less likely than was formerly the case that anyone should be unable to understand the liturgical texts.

The survival of Latin represents the resistance opposed by a written language to the rapid alterations and far-reaching changes of the spoken tongue. It was not inspired by any desire to invest the sacred Action with the veil of mystery.[1]

Similarly the sacred vestments represent merely the survival of a costume originally secular.[2]

Nevertheless the sacred vestments translate the profound intuition of faith that the man who is a priest should vanish

[1] Greek was the original language of the Roman liturgy, as also of Papal documents. Its use continued till about the middle of the third century. Fortescue, *The Mass*. Cf. Allard, op. cit., p. 16.

[2] 'Even in the eighth century the ecclesiastical and the civil garb were still identical', Mgr. Batiffol observes in his *Etudes de Liturgie et D'Archéologie chrétienne*, p. 47. In its essentials the liturgical costume is 'a survival of the Roman secular costume of the fourth century', ibid., p. 83. Cf. Duchesne, *Origines*, p. 402. We can read there Pope Celestine's protest in a letter to the Bishops of the provinces of Vienne and Narbonne against the introduction of a distinctive costume for Bishops and clerics. The protest witnesses, however, to a tendency already in operation, in 428, to distinguish the clergy and laity by their garb. Rome opposed the innovation but finally accepted it under Byzantine influence, especially as regards the pallium. Cf. Batiffol, ibid., pp. 30 and 69. Duchesne, however, attributes the pallium to an imperial grant (*Origines*, pp. 405–407) in Gaul and Spain (ibid., pp. 410–412). The development, however, took the form of retaining and fixing the shape of civil garments which had gone out of use (Duchesne, ibid., p. 402, Batiffol, ibid., p. 83), not inventing special vestments. These remarks obviously concern only the external aspect of the question. The profound significance of the sacred vestments obviously consists in their symbolism. They symbolise the divestment of self and reclothing with Christ. They signify in their fashion that the priest acts in the person of Jesus and that, strictly speaking, he is but the living sacrament of the one priesthood, the priesthood of the eternal Priest who says I in him. They are thus the insignia of that glorious poverty which disappropriates the priest of himself to make him the property of the Word of the Father.

in the Person of the everlasting Priest whose living Sacrament he is. The vesture he wears at the altar symbolises his reclothing with Christ who acts through his ministry.

The ritual of the Mass is easily understood, when we remember that up to the offertory the Mass reproduces in its main lines, the liturgy of the synagogues[1] from which Christianity drew its first converts, the original source of its prayers, lessons and chants,[2] and that from the offertory onwards it develops the words of Consecration, which are Our Saviour's words inserted in a brief account of the Supper.

On the eve of His death Jesus took bread in His holy and venerable hands. This is the offertory with all the prayers of offering both before and after the Preface.

And raising His eyes to Thee, His almighty Father He gave thanks : this is the Preface itself leading up to the Sanctus.

He blessed it : this is the consecration.

He broke it : this is the fraction of the bread.

And He gave it to His disciples : this is the Communion.

The formulas actually in use, though somewhat entangled, constitute nevertheless a perfect unity when they are permitted to live in the soul. But we must of course repeat them, slowly enough to enable the ceremonial acts to communicate all their profound inwardness and all their sober majesty. For we are not concerned with a conventional ceremonial, still less with a magic ritual, but with the most spiritual and most Divine Mystery.

This was the suggestion we sought to convey by the

[1] 'The Christian liturgy is very largely the offspring of the Jewish, in fact simply its continuation.' Duchesne, op. cit., p. 47.
[2] To which may be added the sermon which comments on the lessons.

phrase *Pleroma of the Cross*, which attaches the Liturgy to its true source.

We have borrowed the term—which means accomplishment, supplement, fulfilment, completion—from the Epistle to the Ephesians (i. 23). In this passage St. Paul, speaking of the pre-eminent position of Christ, says that God has put all things beneath His feet and ' has given Him as the Head, above all, of the Church which is His body, the *pleroma* of Him who is wholly fulfilled in all '.

His imagery involves, of itself, this bold designation If the body cannot live without the head, the head itself has its natural complement in the body, and their union is the unity of a single organism.

Moreover, the Apostle, who goes on shortly after to compare the mutual relationship of husband and wife to the relationship between Christ and the Church,[1] undoubtedly had in mind the fact that the Church was born from the Heart of Christ pierced on the Cross, as Eve had been taken from the side of the first Adam. If the Church is the complement of Christ, it is because she has derived from Him all she is and all she gives Him. The mutual dependence therefore is not equal on both sides. For the Church exists only through Christ and has no power save in Him, whereas neither the existence nor the holiness of Christ depends in any way on the existence or holiness of His members.

Nevertheless His function as Saviour remains in a sense merely potential, in a state of expectation so to speak and, as it were, incomplete, until the power of His Passion has actually become the life principle of a humanity which is one body with Himself.

[1] Eph. v. 22–23.

In this aspect the Church is indispensable to Christ, and is a part of His mystic being, in as much as she is the normal term of His redemptive action and the inseparable object of His most intimate love.

The virtue of the Church certainly adds nothing to the virtue of Christ. But it bears witness to it, being its fruit. And since this fruitfulness is the normal expression of the fontal holiness, whose plenitude is the principle of all sanctity, we cannot conceive of Christ being separated without mutilation from the Church.

The Saviour's mission is to save.

This mission, however, *universal de jure*, is only exercised *de facto* to the extent to which mankind answers Christ's appeal and submits to His influence. Therefore the adherence of humanity, soul by soul, as the Mystery of the Church silently unfolds, by continually affording a new outlet to the sanctifying stream dammed up in the Saviour's heart realises in a sense and fulfils His redeeming power. From this point of view the Church is indeed the accomplishment, the fulfilment, the fullness, the *pleroma* of Christ.

The *Mass* bears the same relation to the *Cross*. It realises the Sacrifice it commemorates, and fulfils it by the adherence to it which it effects. It does not claim to reiterate what has been done once for all or renew what is eternal. Its purpose is to open us to the Mystery, and make it present to us by placing us in its presence.

It leads us to the foot of the Cross that Christ's death may find its fulfilment in our death to self, and the wound of *His* Heart bleed in the piercing of ours.

And this was Christ's purpose at the Last Supper: to invest the Church with His Cross by offering her

Communion in His Sacrifice. And if He tasted Himself the Sacrament of His immolation, He did so, it would seem, to communicate with His *Church*, and from this communion draw courage to confront for her sake the agony which was already assaulting His heart.

But the Church on her part could not be without her share of that suffering. Intensely as He might desire to spare us, and though we can truly say in the words of St. Hippolytus's Canon,[1] 'that he stretched out His hands when He suffered to deliver from suffering those who should believe in Him', He could not dispense us from conditions morally indispensable, if we are to attain our true Good.

This supreme Good, which is the grafting of His own life into ours, this infinite gift necessitates by its very immensity the rupture of the self without which the Kingdom of God cannot be established in us.

Therefore it was that on the eve of His death He offered His Apostles and all future believers this food, at once so harsh and so sweet, His crucified Flesh and His outpoured Blood.

He could not offer us less than the food on which He fed Himself, in that mysterious poverty of His human nature wholly appropriated by the Word of God, wholly divested of self. 'My food is to do the will of My Father.'[2] He invited us, as He always invites us, to this poverty in which the dispossession of ourselves will enable Him to say 'I' through our mouths, in our hearts and in our lives. 'This is My Body, this is My Blood.'

What meaning, moreover, could we attach to the

[1] Batiffol, *Leçons sur la Messe*, 8th Edition, p. xv.—Dom Vandeleur, *La Sainte Messe*, 8th Edition, p. 319.
[2] John iv. 34.

appropriation of the Saviour's redeeming death, of which these words are the memorial, if it were not accompanied by a divestment of ourselves proportionate to the growth in us of His mysterious life?

Certainly the efficacy of the sacramental words does not depend upon our dispositions. At every consecration the redemption is set before us, is made truly present in its entire fullness[1] whatever our spiritual state may be.

Nevertheless we shall never truly make that redemption our own except by the *divestment* of self which the words of consecration so powerfully suggest. ' This is My Body, this is My Blood.'

The measure in which this *divestment* is a reality is the measure also of that *reclothing* which is expressed and effected by the *Communion.* It is right to insist upon the objective reality of the Eucharistic Presence. It can indeed never be proclaimed with sufficient gratitude and wonder. Nothing else could bring before us more powerfully what a mystic has dared to call ' the humility of God '[2]; and St. Paul, in even bolder language, ' the annihilation[3] of God '.

But the Source at once all-powerful and annihilated that fills the silence with its mute appeals and holds in its stream, by a self-possession so calm that all its energy seems concentrated in the solitary flame of the little lamp, this source of life-everlasting reveals its mystery only to the humble of heart, the disciples of silence, those who have

[1] This is finely expressed by the Secret for the Ninth Sunday after Pentecost : ' Grant us, we beseech Thee, O Lord, to approach worthily Thy Holy mysteries, for whenever this victim is commemorated, the work of our redemption is carried on.'

[2] Quoted in Maritain, *Art et Scholastique,* p. 245.

[3] The Crampon translation of Phil. ii. 7. ' Il s'est anéanti.' ' He annihilated Himself.' The Westminster Version more literally translates, ' He emptied Himself.' *Author's and translator's note.*

earned to *listen* with the perfect docility of a soul that does, nothing but receive. Such a soul shrinks from speech and not without reason.

Men have in fact too often forgotten that the Eucharistic Presence, though infinitely more real than any local presence, is not a local presence.[1] They have also forgotten that this Presence is given to us under the veil of the species, and that contact with the latter is not of itself contact with the former. The *material* contact with the species is indeed but the sacrament of a *spiritual* contact with the beloved Guest of the soul, that is if the soul is open to the Divine visit.

The ciborium which holds the species is incapable of such a contact, and so is the soul that refuses herself, even though she ' eat and drink her own condemnation, not discerning the Lord's Body '.[2]

It is not, however, our intention to dwell upon the mode, which is indeed ineffable, of the Eucharistic Presence. We shall but express the desire that when men speak of what must always remain ' spirit and life ',[3] their language should be pure from all gross alloy. Our sole purpose has been to portray the Mass as the pleroma of the Cross ; that is as a mystery deriving its entire efficacy from the Sacrifice of the Cross, though it is only by its enactment that the efficacy of that Sacrifice is imparted to us, as the expansion of the redeeming act in the Heart of the Church, identified with the crucified Saviour in the words of the memorial which renders what it commemorates present.

It is, therefore, as impossible to regard the Mass as detracting from the Sacrifice of the Cross, as it is impossible

[1] St. Thomas III, Q. 76, A. 5.   [3] John vi. 63.
[2] I Cor. xi. 29.

to regard the Church Pleroma as detracting from Christ the Head. The redemption, accomplished once for all, is eternally fruitful, provided a genuine adherence to its mystery enables its inexhaustible power to spring up in us. The Liturgy opens the sluices of the river of life, by opening the floodgates of our souls, and makes present to us Calvary's sole and eternal oblation by placing our hearts in its presence. If we might venture a definition, and give the term sacrament the analogical meaning of a sign which in any degree represents and realises supernaturally the Divine,[1] we might define the Sacrifice of the Mass as the Sacrament of the Sacrifice of the Cross, the sign which represents and realises that Sacrifice, the sign which symbolises it and makes it truly present to us, or the sign which symbolises the Sacrifice of the Cross and places us truly, that is spiritually, in its presence. And this definition may itself be summed up in the pregnant formula, moulded on St. Paul's : *The Mass is the Pleroma of the Cross*.

The Mass is a true sacrifice ; it is the sacrifice of the Cross itself, but appropriated by a Church identified with her Head, and by this appropriation providing a channel for its eternal fruitfulness,[2] making its action possible and thus supplying its fulfilment, its plenitude, its pleroma.

It is Christ offering Himself in the Church by a mysterious superposition of sacrifices, the unbloody sacrifice of the Altar being the sacrifice of Calvary in the sacramental acceptance which realises it.

[1] In this case in a supreme degree.

[2] We may, therefore, say that, in a sense, if every grace is derived from the Cross, it also comes to us in a fashion through the Mass, since it is through the Mass that the Cross comes to us and we come to the Cross. We might perhaps express this truth by saying that every grace comes to us from the Cross by the Mass, whether directly and as 'in actu primo' or only indirectly.

The sixth chapter of St. John's Gospel suggests this doctrine with a Divine skill, if we understand it in the sense I shall expound—of the Eucharistic *Sacrifice and Sacrament* taken together, since the spiritual eating of the flesh and blood involves at once our acceptance of the Sacrifice of the Cross, its mystic presence, its accomplishment in us and its fruitfulness in our assimilation to Christ the Host, and moreover the degree to which we adhere to the mystery of the Cross measures exactly its fulfilment in our souls. We hold, in fact, that in this passage St. John is propounding in Eucharistic terms that Communion with the Saviour's Cross whose strict obligation the Synoptists taught,[1] precisely because the Eucharist sacrifice and sacrament is the indispensable leaven which alone can make us adhere to the death of the Son of God and thereby imprint upon us the seal of His Resurrection.

Christ could no doubt have chosen another mode of effecting this appropriation, could have dispensed with the sign, and required only the silent adherence of the heart.

Though always requiring the latter which is indispensable and must be progressively deepened, He has, however, willed that all down the ages a public rite should be at once the symbol and the source of an acceptance of the Sacrifice, in which the sanctification of the Mystical Body should in a sense take precedence in our hearts of our personal sanctification. He has willed that His redemption should always be appropriated by us with the universal reference of its original accomplishment, and that the memorial of His death should have that note of Catholicity which is the mark of true charity.

[1] Matt. x. 38, xvi. 24; Mark viii. 34; Luke ix. 23.

He required this dispossession of self at the heart of prayer, the poverty of spirit which is His first beatitude.

We may perhaps feel a greater sensible attraction to the solemn liturgies of nature or the private recollection of silent prayer. There will be time for both. But we must learn to surrender our personal preferences when they interfere with the performance of our duties.

We owe ourselves to our brothers at this meeting place of common prayer, where the Cross of our Elder Brother is erected in our hearts, a standard of the Divine Brotherhood which is produced by the Fatherhood of God.

How can we be disciples of the great Pauper if we will not be poor even in our relations with Him, if our very prayer is not divested of self, to permit His prayer to arise in our hearts, as the cry of our adoption :

Abba, Pater.

K

3. OPUS DEI[1]

[1] 'The work of God', a term employed to denote the Divine Office in St. Benedict's Rule. See Ch. XLIII, 5.

THE SOUL OF PSALMODY[1]

WORDS are not the only elements of language.

The tone of voice is no less important which inspires them with life and transforms them unceasingly, as our states of mind dictate, by communicating to them something of our own life.

Behind every word spoken there is a person. And even when words attempt to conceal him, the tone of voice immediately betrays his existence and disposition.

Beyond what we say there is what we are. That is why speech always involves a certain music that modifies its contours by investing it with the undertone of our personality.

Words are charged with an atmosphere which reveals what they do not say, what they cannot say, what no one can say, and what is perhaps the essential matter. Words are as much conductors of a psychological current, as vehicles of ideas. They introduce us to a particular aspect of the world and tend to modify our attitude to the world. Very often what endures of a conversation is not so much what we can repeat of it, as the changes it has produced in us. Words have their repercussions and spread out their waves in us, as a stone thrown into the water sets up an undulation, whose circles progressively widen until the impetus is exhausted.

[1] An article published in *La Vie Spirituelle*, September 1934. It is reprinted here with a few unimportant alterations.

Thus language belongs to that order of *symbols* which constitute the underlying reality of the sensible world, in which every being aspires ' beyond '.

Certainly language is more precise, more capable of imparting a definite direction to thought.

But its function is not only to translate discursive thinking, but also to suggest and induce what cannot be said : the Unutterable that is the true reality. We notice that a conversation leaves us depressed or consoled ; always produces in us, however slight the impression it leaves, a sense of pleasure or distaste. We know that the utterance of a word can on occasion plunge us into darkness, or on the contrary kindle a light that will never more be extinguished. But most commonly the most important part of what is said is what is not said, the ' aura ', the atmosphere, all the darkness or light the speaker has admitted.

That is why language is so close to music which is the language of the unspeakable. For the same reason speech so easily turns to song, that the words plunged into the stream which gave them birth and thus in contact with their source may exert all their force and all their power to move us. Music utilises and increases indefinitely the vital rhythm which has already restored to language the concrete vibrations, the living and life-giving heart-beats, of which ideas have been deprived by their abstraction.

It is not therefore surprising that the Christian liturgy has not been able to dispense with the aid of music, and in particular of chant. For its essential purpose is to place us in contact with the eternally living Word that has created the worlds, by whom everything has been made, without whom nothing was made that has been made, and that became flesh and dwelt among us.

Is not in fact the mystery of every word its attachment to that Word and the vestige of It that it retains, the Word that is a Person in a sense infinitely beyond what the term person signifies in human language, the Person of the only Son in the bosom of the Father? If then because of Him everything is in some way ineffable, how much more is not He Himself ineffable?

Human language cannot attempt to express this utterance that is the Word of God without being painfully conscious at every instant of its own limitations, without feeling the need for the flight of song that bears the lark upward in the intoxicated rapture of its rapid ascent to regions closer to the sun.

Language, it is true, to become liturgical, has passed through the fire, has been immeasurably enlarged by the baptism of the Spirit. For it is the words of Scripture that we chant, and our prayer is a biblical prayer. But if in any writing whatsoever the words possess more or less, besides their value as signs, a power of suggestion, in the Bible they become as it were sacraments. This, no doubt, is the key to the entire interpretation of Scripture. The Bible belongs to Pascal's third order, the order of charity, to which only love rooted in faith has access.

This point was most felicitously expressed by the writer of the *Imitation* when he compared the banquet of Scripture to the Eucharistic banquet.[1]

What matters it whether the flour of which the host is baked is of better or worse quality; whether the wheat was grown in one country or in another, whether it has been

[1] Bk. iv. Cap. xi, 4.

ground and baked by the most expert millers and bakers or shows obvious signs of negligence in its preparation? The soul does not feed on these outer appearances. Her gaze is fixed exclusively on the Lord who comes to her beneath the veil of bread. Similarly in Scripture, it is He for whom we must look, Who turns towards us His mysterious Face.

How often we have experienced this as we pondered, in the Missal, passages of Scripture of which we could make very little, whose literal meaning escaped us. Our heart was set on fire by a mysterious encounter. Scripture is a person, Scripture is Jesus. Before as after His advent it is full of Him. Before, it is the night drawing towards the dawn; after, it is the sky brilliant with the midday sun. That is why the piety of Christians has always felt so perfectly at ease in the Old Testament, of which every episode is a window resplendent with the brightness of a single luminary, every page part of a dynamic whole, moving towards Christ.

For this reason also we still chant the psalms, several of which express a Messianic hope so exceeded by its realisation that it would be meaningless to recite them to-day if the light of the Spirit did not reveal beyond the words the reference to Christ.

It is the same always. Scripture can be understood only on our knees, as we feed upon it and become aware of an invisible current of air that moves all its leaves in an unconstrainable aspiration towards the glorious Countenance of Jesus Christ. The true sense of Scripture always lies beyond, beyond the words, the concepts, and the events which are but signs[1] in which faith detects the presence of the *Only Son*.

[1] In a sense sacramental.

But for this very reason, the sacred texts invite the musical development which will make all that is unutterable in them an audible undertone. It was, therefore, a natural development when in the Liturgy they put on the garb of song; and music sought to render the Divine atmosphere with which the words are invested.

Beyond question, psalmody represents the most remarkable of these efforts. It has discovered the secret of opening words without dispersing their spirit, of weaving a sequence of sounds without violating silence, of withdrawing the soul within herself in a most personal prayer while at the same time uniting her to the souls of others in a public prayer, and providing man with the most moving expression of his needs, a supplication which rises above them and crowns with praise the unutterable groans of the Spirit. Nothing is humbler and simpler, more sublime and more spontaneous, more dynamic and more contemplative. There is no *tour de force*, no excitement, not the least attempt at effect, no glance back at self. It is understood that God can never be expressed and that the important matter is to let Him *utter Himself* in the depths of silence, where His Word is engendered.

That is why psalmody *listens* even more than it sings. The body moreover has its share in this work of praise. It is a part which elevates without exciting it, occupies it without distracting it, and rests it without relaxing it. But while the voice follows the words it sings, the soul surrenders herself to the Spirit. And God alone knows what these contacts may achieve.

The seeming monotony of the Chant still further

KI

accentuates the inwardness of the tone, the supreme reserve[1] of faith, and the Divine modesty of love.

Psalmody is, in the sublimest sense of the term, a spiritual music, an interior music at once human and Divine, contemplative and mystical, an act performed in the sphere of the Eucharist and inseparable from it, a sacrament by which Christ prays in the Church for His Father's glory and the salvation of the world.

---

[1] This reserve may be termed miraculous in the authentic Roman liturgy in which the soul is guided with such discretion to her meeting with God that no emotion interferes in advance with its unpredictable novelty. The tact is so perfect, the surrender so unique, that we are compelled to see in it the work of the Holy Spirit and the purest expression of that Christian sacramentalism in which the visible is so completely within the mystery it expresses that it affects us as from within, and in which the ' social ' and the ' collective ' open within our souls the purest spaces of Divine solitude, evoking the most personal and most indescribable converse with the soul's silent Guest.

4. THE LITURGY OF LIFE

THE SPIRIT OF RELIGIOUS VOWS[1]

THERE is but one way to be holy, namely, *to be*. Conscience is *our demand to be*, the voice of being. This is our sole duty, as it is also our sole right, and at bottom our sole desire : *to be*.[2] But though we possess being, we are not Being.

God is Being, the pole star of a compass of which our conscience is the needle. To be, fully, we must therefore give ourselves to Him. This is the centre of our religious vocation, the living rock from which the spring gushes forth. Far from yielding to an illusion and dropping the meat for the shadow, we have, by corresponding with our vocation, but complied scrupulously with the demands of being inscribed in our nature and placed ourselves at the centre of reality. For no creature has any other vocation than to express God, or has being except to give it, to give itself to God and to the entire universe.

God has given us the grace to become so fully conscious of this that we desire to recognise it explicitly and carry it out in our lives. It is not, however, God's plan to deprive us of the being He has given. On the contrary, ' God created beings to exist ', and he communicated to them, so far as their nature permitted, the privilege of His own Being, namely to be a pure gift by the infinite ecstasy of eternal charity.

[1] An article published in *La Vie Spirituelle*, October 1, 1933.
[2] ' To be or not to be, that is the question ', we might say, giving another meaning to Shakespeare's words.

God has therefore called us to exercise this privilege : to make our being a gift.

To give ourselves to God is, in short, to transfer our self to Him ; *to adopt God as our self.* The love of charity, that is to say, tends with its entire weight towards God as its centre, and inclines us to be in relation to God in His undivided Trinity what each Divine Person is in relation to the Other : ' That all may be one *in us*, even as Thou and I are one.'[1]

' This is holiness : to be a living relation to God. Henceforward *it is not I who live*, it is Christ who liveth in me.'[2]

That is why *Jesus* is pre-eminently the Holy One : ' *Tu solus Sanctus*.' His sacred humanity had no need like ours to be divested and disappropriated of its self. It is in a state of donation, wholly referred to the Word in whom it subsists, that He may express Himself personally in it.

The love of charity, which in our souls is a filial love, is also, however, in its fashion a love of equality, of reciprocity. God loves us with a paternal, as we love Him with a filial, love. And He transfers His life into us as we ours into Him. ' In that day you shall know that I am in the Father and you in Me, and I in you.'[3] God lives our life as we live His, according to the measure of our love.

But what measure of love can we offer to infinite love, save a measure which is measureless ? We have therefore to expand boundlessly our capacity to love.

The evangelical counsels have no other object. The counsels are the wings of charity. Their sole aim is to

[1] John xvii. 21–22.   [2] Gal. ii. 20.   [3] John xiv. 20.

mature all the powers of our being for this transference of love, to subject all we possess to God's good pleasure. To give them a purely negative interpretation would be to falsify their meaning completely. They aim at life, as does every thing which proceeds from the life-giving *Spirit*.

Saint Benedict expressed the entire mystery of *poverty* in this brief saying : 'Regard all the utensils of the monastery as sacred vessels.'[1]

The visible world is in our hands like the bread multiplied by Jesus' love. We must not let a fragment of it be lost. Nothing is more remote from the genuinely Christian spirit than contempt for corporeal things which are as much God's creatures as are the angelic orders. The spirit of poverty is but an immense love and a boundless reverence. Precisely because these things are Divine in their origin, they must remain such in our use of them and provide material to build in ourselves the city of God, furnish us with the stones of the altar and oil for the lamp. It is to God that we must surrender the ownership of all, using for our own profit only what is needed to make us fit instruments of His will. We should, however, understand this minimum without scruple or nicety, with a flexible adaptation to the requirements of our circumstances. Nor should we lose sight of the generosity and the large-hearted munificence which befit children of the King of kings.

'To treat as sacred vessels' all the temporal goods of which we make use, is, therefore, to behold them with that vision of faith and love which reveals the sacramental nature of the humblest objects. With what reverence and gratitude should we sit at a table at which we are God's guests. With what care and delicacy we should administer

[1] Rule XXXI, 19, 20, ed. Butler, p. 62.

the patrimony entrusted to us by the heavenly Father for the benefit of His children, with what generosity and simplicity we should impart to our brethren goods which are His in the hands of others, as in our own.

Poverty is not contempt for earthly goods but their sublimation and emancipation. It gives matter wings that the whole of reality may sing. 'All realities will sing, nothing else will.'

Chastity is no less fruitful. Not only has God given us being, He has also given us the power to give being. He has made us participate in His creative power, and entrusted to us the dispensation of life. He has put into our hands the fate of an innumerable posterity to which our love can give birth, and has made our bodies sacraments of this Divine power.

God, who is father and mother infinitely, for the infinite Good that He is, is infinitely eager to lavish itself, has made us fathers and mothers of a multitude without number. It is therefore utterly false that our vow of chastity is a refusal, something negative. On the contrary its object is to enable us to realise *explicitly*, so far as a human being is capable of it, the entire infinity and universality of God's fatherhood and motherhood. What delights mothers' hearts in their little children is that inner world which is the secret of their being and the indescribably mysterious unfolding of the Divine life in them. The true end of generation is the birth of God in the newly created soul. Unfortunately this sacramental function of the flesh is too often lost sight of, and the baby's bodily needs make parents forget the divine vocation of its soul. It is for us to bear it in mind and supply what so many parents are unable to give by gathering together in our souls the souls of all those children for whose birth to the Spirit no one has taken care, to offer them to their Father as a victim of praise in a heart full of the love of Mother Church.

But this is not enough. Our love must be in the fullest sense catholic, embracing all men and brooding over all souls. Fathers and mothers overburdened with domestic cares and in bondage to material needs require fathers and mothers of their mental life and the life of their hearts. They need to lay down their burden and share its weight with us. They must always be able to count upon our prayers, our sympathy, our charity and truly find in us ' the mild and joyous countenance of Jesus Christ '.[1]

Moreover, Christian families are not their own end. They are subordinated to the Catholic unity of the Church. Each of their members must therefore be made a member of this universal family, incorporated into the mystical Body of Christ. This universal family is committed to our charge ; it is for us to generate the mystical Christ.

We recall the fertility promised to Abraham : ' Behold the sky and, if thou canst, count the stars : so numerous shall be thy posterity.'[2] How we must widen our hearts to receive all these children who, so the Father's love has willed, should be unceasingly born of our charity. What love we should have for them, and what a Divine passion should consume consecrated souls in whom every human creature has a right to hear the heart-beats of Jesus. To be father and mother of every human being—as is God Himself —and offer each the refuge of a love capable of giving itself wholly to all, because entirely divested of self, this is the true purpose of the vow of chastity. ' The righteous man,' said the Psalmist, ' will flourish like the palm tree; will spread out his branches like the cedar of Libanus.'[3]

[1] *Ordo Commendationis Animae*, 3rd Prayer.   [2] Gen. xv. 5.   [3] Ps. xci. 13.

If, however, we should love objects because they reflect God's light, and have a passion for souls that we may bring His life to birth in them, we must love before all things and with a unique attachment the God who is our reason for loving everything and everybody else.

Obedience mounts guard over the holy of holies, which is purity of intention and virginity of heart. For it is always in a virgin heart that the Word makes His abode, a heart in which the *Self* has not contrived a lurking place and of whose every beat the Spirit can take possession. That is why more than all our works or all our successes God values our unreserved obedience. For before giving us His creation He wishes to give first of all Himself, to pour into us the fullness of His life, before making its superabundance overflow upon others. Obedience insures the freedom of these Divine invasions. Authority is the sacrament of *our* purity of intention, and the instrument of our genuine liberty. Certainly we are by no means obliged to think that our superiors' decisions are infallibly the wisest, though it would be conceited to think that they are more often mistaken than ourselves. But the object of obedience is not to make us perform the most perfect outward actions but so to keep ourselves in God's hand that He may be able to express Himself in us *beyond* anything we are capable of understanding or doing.

We shall thus cease to be slaves of our actions and work, while performing them better, for the sake of the majesty of Jesus Christ who does them in us and lives our life.[1]

Lending ourselves to all things, but imprisoning our-

---

[1] 'Perform small actions as well as great ones for the sake of Jesus Christ who does them in us and lives our life. Then great and small are alike easy because of His omnipotence.' Pascal, *Mystère de Jésus*, Br. 553.

selves in none, surpassing the fidelity of our hands by the adherence of our heart to the one thing necessary, we shall be able to preserve the sacramental vision of things which makes all that is Divine in it shine in a dew-drop, and links all the actions to which our duty obliges us, as successive stages of the great Liturgy which ' by the unity of our thought and the harmony of our love[1] hymns Jesus Christ ' with the Holy Ghost to the glory of the Father.

Undoubtedly there is but one way of being holy, namely to be. But for us to be is to allow God to be in us all that He is in Himself and all that He wills to be in us, and take such possession of all our powers that He can say I in our life : ' This is *My* body. This is *My* Blood.'

This is finely expressed by the following excerpt from a dialogue between Our Lord and Jean de Quintanadoine, who introduced into France St. Theresa's Carmelite Reform (Died 1634) :

' O Lord, what a loss it is not to serve Thee. What a loss indeed. May I serve Thee, My God.'

' What prevents your serving Me ? '

' I am my own hindrance . . . O Lord, it is now a long time since I offered Thee my body, my soul—since they belong to Thee, take them.'

' John, since they are Mine, and you have given them to Me, I accept them as My property. *And* now I am going to entrust them to you again, not as your own but as my possession.'

' O Lord, grant me Thy grace and I shall live, not as my own possession, but as Thine and for Thee.'[2]

Our life is thus put back into our hands as Christ's deposit. How shall we live it on the level of His heart,

---

[1] Cf. Ignatius of Antioch, Letter to the Ephesians, iv. 1.
[2] Brèmond, *Literary History of Religious Thought*, Vol. II, p. 279.

save by living it in Him? Our mute gaze must never be weary of questioning the beloved Guest of the soul, that He may show us His will and perform it in us.

Thus the rule and the measure of our action will be also its source and end, and all summed up in a word: *Jesus*.

Jesus, however, is inseparable from the Church.[1] The mystery of Jesus is unfolded in the Mystery of the Church, as the sun multiplies its fires in the colours of a stained window.

To live for Jesus, is to live in the Church. We belong to the Church, and, like the altar vessels, all our faculties are dedicated to God's service.

Our entire life is a liturgy and our humblest actions magnified by the universal resonance given to them by the necessarily Catholic mission[2] with which the Church has invested us.

Nothing should seem petty in a life called to such a universal influence, and certain of exercising it, if it wills to do so. What can disturb the peace of a soul completely surrendered? Unless we ourselves abandon the struggle, failure is impossible where the sole condition of success is love.

But shall we be loyal to love?

Since the Prince of the Apostles broke his oath of allegiance, can we flatter ourselves that we shall keep ours?

---

[1] The entire mystery of the Church is contained in the words spoken to Saul on the road to Damascus: 'I am Jesus whom thou persecutest.' Acts ix. 5. The Church is indeed the mysterious sacrament of the blessed poverty which dispossesses us of self to make us a living Host in the hands of the great Pauper. 'I am Jesus.' How indispensable it is to return to this sublime theology and behold the Church with the eyes of faith as a Mystery as invisible to the eyes of the flesh as the mystery of the Blessed Trinity. Are they not in fact the same mystery? 'I am Jesus.'

[2] Catholic means universal.

The Mercy which made him the unshakable rock on which the Church is built can also prevent the consequences of our weakness. It was when he trusted his own strength that the Apostle succumbed to the jeers of a servant girl. When he relied upon his Lord he was able to defy an empire. And we are still living upon his victory. ' When thou wast young, thou didst gird thyself and didst walk whither thou wouldest ; but when thou shalt be old thou shalt stretch forth thy hands, and another shall gird thee and lead thee whither thou wouldst not.'[1]

What is required is not so much to act as to allow God to act, by surrendering ourselves to the creative embrace of the Power ' that mercifully compels even our rebellious wills '.[2] ' Receive me, O Lord, according to Thy promise, and I shall live.'[3]

Saul knew the happy moment when the soul, struck down by mercy and taken captive by love, has no other resource than surrender. ' Lord, what wilt Thou have me do ? '[4]

It is then in this spirit that we must renew our vows, in order to free ourselves from the burden of ourselves and lose ourselves in the depths of Being and Love.

Then we shall understand that the counsels are the wings of charity, and that we have not received a spirit of bondage unto fear but the spirit of adoption of sons whereby we cry : *Abba, Pater.* Our Father.[5]

[1] John xxi. 18.
[2] Secret for the Fourth Sunday after Pentecost.
[3] Ps. cxviii. (Vulgate).
[4] Acts ix. 6 (Clementine edition of the Vulgate).
[5] Rom. viii. 15.

5. THE SONG OF THE POVERELLO

THE CANTICLE OF THE SUN

Most high, most mighty, good Lord,
to Thee be praise, glory, honour and all blessing,
to Thee alone, Most High, do they belong,
and no man is worthy to invoke Thy name.

Praise be to Thee, my Lord, with all Thy creatures;
Especially my lord, brother Sun,
who brings day and Thou dost give light through him;
and he is beautiful and radiant, and of great splendour.
He signifies Thee, Most High.

Praise be to Thee, my Lord, for sister moon and the stars,
in the heavens Thou hast fashioned them bright and precious
and fair.

Praise be to Thee, my Lord, for our brother the wind,
and for the air, the clouds, for calm and all weathers
by whom Thou dost sustain all creatures in life.

Praise be to Thee, my Lord, for sister water,
who is very serviceable to us, humble, precious and chaste.

Praise be to Thee, my Lord, for brother fire,
by whom Thou givest us light in the night;
and he is handsome and joyous, sturdy and strong.

Praise be to Thee, my Lord, for the earth, our sister and
mother,
who doth sustain and govern us,
and brings forth divers fruits and flowers of many colours
and grass.

Praise ye and bless my Lord.
Give Him thanks and serve Him with great humility.

6. THE UNIVERSAL PRAYER

THOU SHALT LOVE

An address on the Soul of Psalmody was transmitted by wireless at the Gregorian Triduum, held in St. Joseph's Church, Geneva, on January 25th, 26th, and 28th, 1934, under the presidency of M. William Montillet. We reproduce here the second part of the address.

How can a single soul be debarred from the intercession of the sacred Liturgy, be excluded from this prayer which is the Catholic, that is, the universal prayer.

Surely we should be filled with joy and hope when we consider that the same or similar texts, drawn from the same Book, are sung in all the Orthodox and Anglican cathedrals and religious houses, as they are also sung in all the churches of the Protestant bodies, while our Hebrew brethren still recite them in the language of their Fathers— who are also ours—beneath the walls of Sion.

Thus a certain universality has been already realised by prayer, which tends towards an increasingly perfect inner union and should ultimately produce that external unity whose merciful obligation is imposed by the fact of a public revelation.

We may not, however, forget the vast populations taught by Brahmanism, Buddhism or Islam, nor any of those isolated individuals who are unattached to any Church, belong to no denomination but are nevertheless *called* like their brethren—men and women whose sincerity has already made them children of the Spirit. Many of them lament this disunion which condemns human energies

305

to a barren dispersion. Many desire an alliance of all the spiritual forces, a common front of all men of good will against whatever renders human life unworthy of man and unworthy of God. Many are but waiting for a call to reply : ' here.'

God grant they may know how deeply we share these aspirations, and that we regard this disunion as a sin, for which the responsibility is very largely ours.

And may they permit us to remind them that according to the teaching of Christianity, good will, which since it is the unlimited receptiveness of a spirit completely open to the light, always involves at least an implicit adherence to the Mystery of Jesus in the Church,[1] is the sole strictly indispensable condition for the Redemption of the individual and the human race. If each one of us yields himself at every step to the Light that is in him, if he *does* the truth, does his utmost to secure the *triumph* in all his actions private and public, in his country, as in his home, in his relations with others as in his relations with himself, of what he sincerely believes to be the intention of the *Spirit*, he performs, to the extent of his capacity, his task as a man, and assists in the most fruitful and most indispensable way the advent of God's Kingdom ; ' for God is spirit, and they who adore Him, must adore Him in spirit and in truth '.[2]

In the last resort the future of humanity will be decided by what the individual has resolved in the bottom of his heart.

' Every soul that raises itself, raises the world.'

[1] To the great mystery of Poverty. Cf. Mark ii. 14 and Mark ix. 40.
[2] John iv. 24.

It is from within, by an increase of the spiritual life in each individual, that the unity for which we are all longing will be achieved. For the Kingdom of God is within us. That is why we are all invited by the Magnificat antiphon[1] we are about to chant, in which we can hear the disconsolate complaint of all the unemployed and the still more heart-rending lament of those who have lost faith in the value of life and ask themselves what can be the worth of their existence and the meaning of their efforts.

The father of the family said to those who would become his labourers : ' Why stand you all the day idle ? ' And they replied : ' Because no man hath hired us.' ' Go,' he said, ' into my vineyard, and whatever is just I will pay you.'

The end of life is not to produce unremittingly fresh external wealth—however useful, urgent and a matter of duty—in short, however necessary it may be, and in fact is, to improve the lot of the majority.

The end of life is to fulfil man's spiritual vocation, which is to become a child of God.

That which constitutes man's inviolable dignity, which renders slavery a disgrace, war madness, and selfishness in all its forms an apostasy, is that every human being, be he a new-born babe but an hour old, or an incurable lunatic, possesses an unlimited capacity to respond, here or beyond the veil, to infinite Love who has created us because He would make us, in His likeness, beings of love, and has given us this single commandment, sealed by the blood of His Only Son :

Thou shalt love

[1] For Septuagesima. It was the text of the address.

The chapters of this third part may be spiritually connected in the following order:

(1) The Fruitfulness of the Mystery.
(2) The Theology of the Mystery.
(3) The Shrine of the Mystery.
(4) The Guardians of the Mystery.
(5) The Singer of the Mystery.
(6) The Catholicity (universality) of the Mystery.